CENSUS COPIES AND INDEXES IN THE LIBRARY OF THE SOCIETY OF GENEALOGISTS

compiled by Else Churchill

Published by the
Society of Genealogists
14 Charterhouse Buildings
Goswell Road
London EC1M 7BA

First published 1987 as
*Census Indexes in the Library of
the Society of Genealogists*
Second edition 1990

Third edition 1997

© Society of Genealogists 1997

ISBN 1 85951 070 1

CONTENTS

Introduction		v
Abbreviations		vii
ENGLAND		
BEDFORDSHIRE	BE	1
BERKSHIRE	BK	1
BUCKINGHAMSHIRE	BU	3
CAMBRIDGESHIRE	CA	6
CHESHIRE	CH	7
CORNWALL	CO	8
CUMBERLAND	CU	10
DERBYSHIRE	DB	11
DEVONSHIRE	DE	14
DORSET	DO	17
DURHAM	DU	18
ESSEX	ES	20
GLOUCESTERSHIRE	GL	22
HAMPSHIRE	HA	24
HEREFORDSHIRE	HE	25
HERTFORDSHIRE	HR	26
HUNTINGDONSHIRE	HU	27
KENT	KE	28
LANCASHIRE	LA	30
LEICESTERSHIRE	LE	36
LINCOLNSHIRE	LI	37
LONDON/MIDDLESEX	MX	40
NORFOLK	NF	43
NORTHAMPTONSHIRE	NH	45
NORTHUMBERLAND	NB	46
NOTTINGHAMSHIRE	NT	48
OXFORDSHIRE	OX	50
RUTLAND	RU	52
SHROPSHIRE	SH	53
SOMERSET	SO	55
STAFFORDSHIRE	ST	56
SUFFOLK	SF	58
SURREY	SR	59
SUSSEX	SX	61
WARWICKSHIRE	WA	63
WESTMORLAND	WE	66
WILTSHIRE	WL	67
WORCESTERSHIRE	WO	74
YORKSHIRE	YK	75
CHANNEL ISLANDS	CI	86
ISLE OF MAN	IM	86
ROYAL NAVY		87
IRELAND	IR	87
SCOTLAND	SC	92
WALES	WS	100
OVERSEAS		108
APPENDIX - Further reading		117

INTRODUCTION

The Society produced the second edition of its guide to the census records held in its library in 1990. Originally the guide listed the returns or indexes for each parish or place within a county, but did not show the shelf location.

At this time few censuses had been fully indexed but much work was in progress. Most local Family History Societies had commenced work on indexing the 1851 census in some way but few, if any, were complete when the second edition was published. The standards of the indexes varied considerably. Some societies opted to produce surname and folio indexes only, while others extended the scope to include full name, age and place of birth. Sometimes the indexes were for parishes only while others covered a complete Registration District. Occasionally the returns were fully transcribed. This guide does not distinguish between the types of indexes held but does try to show the area covered.

Gradually the Federation of Family History Societies and the Public Record Office (PRO) produced guidelines for indexing. The LDS Church/Genealogical Society of Utah (GSU) co-ordinated and funded a project to transcribe and index the whole of the 1881 census and subsequently produced this work on microfiche. Their work has revolutionised the way family historians now approach their research and has set standards for others to follow when producing finding aids for the census returns. Before commencing work on the 1881 census the GSU undertook pilot projects on three counties to transcribe and index the whole of the 1851 census. They have donated these pilot project indexes for Devon, Norfolk and Warwickshire to the Society and they are listed in the guide.

Over the years many more census indexes have been produced. Not only is the 1881 census fully transcribed and indexed for each county (and a national index is due) but all counties have something for 1851. Many counties have been completely indexed for 1851 and some, notably Oxfordshire, Lincolnshire and Nottinghamshire have produced indexes for later and earlier censuses. Oxfordshire FHS has provided hard copy of its 1851 census index transcripts and indexes as well as a computerised version of the index for the whole county.

Prior to its transfer to the Family Record Centre, the Public Record Office donated more than 2000 films of original census returns, mainly for the years 1841, 1851 and 1861. These returns are held in the Lower Library and listed in this guide by District and Piece Number.

HOW TO USE THIS GUIDE - ENGLAND and WALES 1841-1891

The sheer wealth of census indexes, transcripts and copies of original returns obtained by the Society since publication of the earlier editions means that the previous arrangement of the guide by parish is now impractical and would run to several hundred pages. The original returns for England and Wales were arranged by Registration Districts, Sub Districts and Enumeration Districts and most indexers have followed this arrangement as does this guide. Thus establishing in which Registration District your ancestors would have lived is essential.

The Society has gazetteers, census place indexes and census class lists which can be used to work this out. These are listed in the England and Wales reading list and can be found at the Middle Library Enquiry Counter. Once the Registration District is known, turn to the appropriate county page where the Society's holdings are listed. As most of the 1851 returns are held and have indexes, all the 1851 Registration Districts for the county are noted. Remember that Registration

Districts often cross county boundaries and this is shown in the listings of indexes and returns held. The PRO Piece Number, Volume Number of the Index (if appropriate) and the location of the Society's holdings are shown in the guide.

For the censuses after 1851, unless stated otherwise, only those Registration Districts for which the Society holds returns or indexes are listed.

Certain counties have been transcribed or indexed purely by parish and are not arranged by Registration District or it is felt that the indexing of the Registration District is complicated. Where this is the case, a parish list has been made which will assist in identifying an index or transcription for a particular place - see the holdings listed for Buckinghamshire, Shropshire, Warwickshire and Wiltshire. Yorkshire has been divided into the three Ridings but arranged by Registration District.

PRE-1841 CENSUS

Decennial censuses were taken from 1801 but those prior to 1841 were head counts arranged by parish. A few nominal lists were made and have survived. The Society holds many copies of these along with what might be considered census substitutes which list the population of a place by name and often give other details. There are guides to these records listed in the reading list and the Society's holdings are listed in this guide.

2% CENSUS SAMPLE

A large number of computer transcripts were made of the 1851 census. The major part of this data is a 2% sample of the census books of England, Scotland and Wales, the researchers transcribing every fiftieth book. The transcripts were originally compiled by Professor Michael Anderson and published by Chadwick Healy Ltd on microfiche. An index to the 450,159 individuals listed in the sample and a few other transcripts (including many institutions) was made by Dr Alan Stanier and published jointly with the Society of Genealogists in 1990. The Society holds copies of both the sample and its index on microfiche. The parishes covered are listed in this guide.

IRELAND, SCOTLAND and OVERSEAS

The censuses were arranged by parish or place and are listed as such in the guide. The Irish returns prior to 1901 were destroyed although a few fragments may survive and are described in guides in the reading lists. Those which the Society holds along with what might be considered census substitutes are listed. Many microfilm copies of original returns for Scotland have been obtained through the Society's sponsorship scheme and all films held are listed. There are also pre-1841 census lists and census substitutes for Scotland. At the time of publication the Society does not hold the GSU/SRO Transcription and Indexes for the Scottish 1881 Census, nor does it have the National Index. Several overseas Societies have kindly donated indexes to the Society and various returns are found in periodicals. These are listed by place in the guide.

Many people assisted with this edition. Thanks are due to Sue Spurgeon who sorted the text of the second edition with exports from the current computer catalogue to provide parish listings. A team of volunteers added shelf mark and locations to the text. Nicholas Newington-Irving scanned periodicals and oversaw the compilation of the Scottish, Irish and overseas sections. Neville Taylor edited the text.

Else Churchill

ABBREVIATIONS

AIH = All-Ireland Heritage
Am = American
Archl = Archaeological
AUAn = Australian
BIJ = British and Irish Journal of the British FHS of Los Angeles
Bull = Bulletin
C = (after a date) century or (in shelf mark) Censuses section of county or country
Carib = Caribbeana
cen = census
cens = censuses
CGSQ = California Genealogical Society Quarterly
civ = Civil
Co = County
CRS = Catholic Record Society
dist = District
distrbn = Distribution
E = East
exc = excluding
ext = Extracts
ff = folio
FH = Family History
FHn = Family Historian
FHS = Family History Society
Forum = The Genealogical Forum of Portland, Oregon Monthly/Quarterly Bulletin
G = (in shelf mark) General section of county or country
Gencal = Genealogical
Gengst = Genealogist
Genlgy = Genealogy
GPV = Griffith's Primary Valuation of Ireland
GSU = Genealogical Society of Utah
Hist = History
IoW = Isle of Wight
Ir = Irish
Is = Island(s)
J = Journal
L = (in shelf mark) Local section of county or country
Lib = Library
Loc = Local
Mag = Magazine
Memoires = Memoires de Société Généalogique Canadienne-Française
Mf = Microfilm <Lower library>

Mfc = Microfiche <Apply to staff - unless otherwise stated>
MIG = Migration
MLC = Middle Library Counter
Mother Lode = The Mother Lode-Ore/ Golden Roots of the Mother Lode
N = North
NE = New England
NEHGR = The New England Historical and Genealogical Register
NGSQ = National Genealogical Society Quarterly
NandQ = Notes and Queries
N/L = Newsletter
NLI = National Library of Ireland
NYRecord = The New York Genealogical and Biographical Record
OAP = Old Age Pension
Occ = Occasional
parly = Parliamentary
PER = Periodicals
prot = Protestant
pt = Part
Pub = Publication
Q = Quarterly
R = (in shelf mark) Registers section of county or country
RC = Roman Catholic section of the Religions shelves
RD = Registration District
Ref = Reference
Reg = Register
Res = Research
ret = Return
S = South
SCH = Schools shelves
SD = Sub-district
ser = Series
Soc = Soc
SP = Summer Palace
SRO = Scottish Records Office
Sq = Square
St = Saint
svy = Survey
Terr = Territory
tp = Township
Trans = Transactions
Val = Valley
vol = Volume
W = West

ENGLAND

BEDFORDSHIRE (BE)

1767 BE papist return (CRS Occ Paper 2) [RC/PER]
1782 Cardington census (BE Hist Rec Soc 52) [BE/PER]
1788 Milton Ernest, Podington & Hinwick & Thurleigh census (BE FHS J 6/3) [BE/PER]

BEDFORDSHIRE **1841**
Censearch index to its own unpublished transcript - county complete [Mfc]

BEDFORDSHIRE **1851**
Bedfordshire FHS 1851 Census Index Vols 1-8 [BEF]
County Complete.   * = Microfilm held

REGISTRATION DISTRICT	HO 107	Volume No	Location
Ampthill RD	1754*	BEF 4	BE/C 2
Bedford RD	1751-1752*	BEF 1-2, 8	BE/C 1,4
Biggleswade RD	1753*	BEF 3	BE/C 2
Leighton Buzzard RD	1756*	BEF 6	BE/C 3
Luton RD	1757*	BEF 7	BE/C 4
Woburn RD	1755*	BEF 5	BE/C 3
Hitchin RD - Bedfordshire part	1743*	BEF 4	BE/C 2
Huntingdon RD - Bedfordshire part	1750*	BEF 2/1	BE/C 1
Wellingborough RD - Bedfordshire part	1710*	BEF 1/2	BE/C 1

BEFORDSHIRE **1861**
REGISTRATION DISTRICT   RG 9   * = Microfilm held
Ampthill RD - Shillington & *part* Ampthill SDs   0999-1000*
Bedford RD   0985-0993*
Biggleswade RD   0994-0998*
Caxton RD   1017*
Leighton Buzzard RD - Eddlesborough SD   1005-1009*
Luton RD   1010-1015*

BEDFORDSHIRE **1881**
GSU Transcripts & Indexes - county complete   [Lower Library Mfc]

BERKSHIRE (BK)

1767 BK papist return (CRS Occ Paper 2) [RC/PER]
1801 Binfield census [BK/C 4 or (BK FHS Mag 3/2-4) BK/PER]
1821 Caversham census: *see Oxfordshire*

BERKSHIRE **1841**
Berkshire & Oxfordshire 1841 Census Index - Oxfordshire FHS [OXF]
REGISTRATION DISTRICT   HO 107
Abingdon RD   0020, 0024, 0032   OXF [Mfc]
Wallingford RD   0023, 0030, 0025   OXF [Mfc]

Censearch index to its own unpublished transcript - county complete [Mfc]

BERKSHIRE **1851**
Berkshire FHS 1851 Census Index Vols 1-12 [BKF]
County Complete. * = Microfilm held

REGISTRATION DISTRICT	HO 107	Volume No	Location
Abingdon RD	1688*	BKF 4	BK/C2
Bradfield RD	1691*	BKF 7	BK/C 2
Cookham RD	1694*	BKF 10	BK/C 2
Easthampstead RD	1694*	BKF 11	BK/C 2
Faringdon RD	1687*	BKF 2	BK/C 2
Hungerford RD	1686*	BKF 11	BK/C 2
Newbury RD	1685*	BKF 1	BK/C 2
Reading RD	1692*	BKF 8	BK/C 2
Wallingford RD	1690*	BKF 6	BK/C 2
Wantage RD	1689*	BKF 5	BK/C 2
Windsor RD	1695*	BKF 12	BK/C 2
Wokingham RD	1693*	BKF 9	BK/C 2
Basingstoke RD - Berkshire part	1681*	BKF 9	BK/C 2
Henley RD - Berkshire part	1725	BKF 9	BK/C 2
Oxford RD - Berkshire part	1728*	BKF 4/2	BK/C 2

BERKSHIRE **1851 2% Sample** [surname index] [Mfc]
   Bucklebury; Cumnor; Embourne; Fernham; Isley West

BERKSHIRE **1861**
REGISTRATION DISTRICT   RG 9   * = Microfilm held, county complete
Abingdon RD   0730-0735*
Bradfield RD   0742-0744*
Cookham RD   0753-0754*
Easthampstead RD   0755-0757*
Faringdon RD   0727-0729*
Hungerford RD   0723-0726*
Newbury RD   0719-0722*
Reading RD   0745-0749*
Wallingford RD   0739-0741*
Wantage RD   0736-0738*
Windsor RD   0758-0761*
Wokingham RD   0750-0752*

BERKSHIRE **1871**
Berkshire & Oxfordshire 1871 Census Index - Oxfordshire FHS [OXF]

REGISTRATION DISTRICT	RG 10		Location
Abingdon RD	1261-1266	OXF	Mfc
Wallingford RD	1272-1274	OXF	Mfc

BERKSHIRE **1881**
GSU Transcripts & Indexes - county complete [Lower Library Mfc]

BERKSHIRE **1891**
Berkshire & Oxfordshire 1891 Census Index - Oxfordshire FHS [OXF]

REGISTRATION DISTRICT	RG 12		Location
Abingdon RD	977-981	OXF	Mfc
Farringdon RD	974-976	OXF	Mfc
Wallingford RD	985-986	OXF	Mfc

Wantage RD	982-984	OXF	Mfc
Banbury RD - Berkshire part	1180-1184	OXF	Mfc
Henley RD - Berkshire part	1156-1159	OXF	Mfc
Oxford RD - Berkshire part	1267-1269	OXF	Mfc

BUCKINGHAMSHIRE [BU]

1750 Lower Winchendon census [BU/C 1]
1767 BU papist return (CRS Occ Paper 2) [RC/PER]
1801 Wooburn census [BU/C 1]
1821 Princes Risborough census [Apply to Staff (Shelf 9)]
1831 Princes Risborough census [Apply to Staff (Shelf 9)]

BUCKINGHAMSHIRE **1841**
Bletchley [BU/C 1]
Fenny Stratford [BU/C 1]
Filgrave [BU/C 1]
Gayhurst [BU/C 1]
Hardmead [BU/C 1]
Hitcham [BU/C 1]
Walton [BU/C 1]
Water Eaton [BU/C 1]
Wollstone Great & Little [BU/C 1]
Woughton on the Green [BU/C 1]

BUCKINGHAMSHIRE **1851**
Buckinghamshire FHS 1851 Census Transcript & Index [BUF]; Bletchley Archaeological &
Historical Society 1851 Census Surname Index [BAS]   * = Microfilm held

REGISTRATION DISTRICT	HO 107	Volume No	Location
Amersham RD	1717	BAS	BU/C 1
Amersham RD [ff578-689]	1717	BUF 2.5	Mfc
Amersham RD			
- Beaconsfield SD [ff624-685]	1717		BU/C 1
Aylesbury RD *part**	1721	BUF 5.1.1-3	Mfc
[ff5-232,245-735]		BUF 5.2.1	Mfc
		5.3 & 5.4.1-3	Mfc
Aylesbury RD			
- Aylesbury SD [ff236-421]	1721*		BU/C 1
Buckingham RD *part* [ff214-219,285-357]	1724	BUF 8.2.2	Mfc
Eton RD	1718	BUF 3.1.1-3	Mfc
		BUF 3.2.1-3	Mfc
		BUF 3.3.1-3	Mfc
Newport Pagnell RD	1723	BAS	BU/C 1
- Newport Pagnell *part*	1723	BUF 7.1.2	Mfc
[ff 56-123,482-575,692-734]		BUF 7.3.1	Mfc
		BUF 7.3.2	Mfc
		BUF 7.3.4	Mfc
Newport Pagnell RD			
- Newport Pagnell & Olney SDs	1723	BUF 7.2.1 &	
[ff 348-370 & 579-602]		BUF 7.3.1	BU/C 1
Winslow RD	1722		
Wycombe RD *part* [ff4-75,322-528]	1719*	BUF 4.1.1	Mfc
		BUF 4.1.3	Mfc
		BUF 4.2.1-2	Mfc
Wycombe RD *part* [ff4-86, 289-575, 656-687]	1720	BUF 4.3.1	Mfc
		BUF 4.4.1-3	Mfc
		BUF 7.3.1	Mfc
		BUF 6.5.3	Mfc

Bicester RD
 - Buckinghamshire part [ff257-263]   1729   BUF 11.1   Mfc
Leighton Buzzard RD
 - Buckinghamshire part [ff372-385]   1756*   BUF 14.3   Mfc
Leighton Buzzard RD *part* [ff491-511] 1756*   BUF 14.4   BU/C 1
Berkhampstead RD - Berkshire part   1716   BUF 1   Mfc
Brackley RD   1735   BUF 12   Mfc
Pottersbury RD - Berkshire part   1737   BUF 13.1 & 1.1 Mfc

BUCKINGHAMSHIRE **1851** PARISHES COVERED SO FAR:
Buckinghamshire FHS 1851 Census Indexes [BUF]; Oxfordshire FHS 1851Census Indexes [OXF]; Windsor, Slough & District FHS journal [Heritage]

Amersham BU/C 1
Ashendon BUF 5.1.2 Mfc
Asheridge BU/C 1
Ashley Green BU/C 1
Aston Clinton BUF 5.3 Mfc
Aston Abbotts BUF 5.4.1 Mfc
Aston Sandord 5.2.1 Mfc
Astwood BU/ C 1 & BUF 7.3.1 Mfc
Ayelsbury BU/C 1
Beaconsfield BU/C 1
Bellingdon BU/C 1
Bletchley BU/C 1
Boarstall BUF11.1 Mfc
Botley BU/C1
Bow Brickhill BU/C 1 & BUF 7.1.2 Mfc
Bradwell Abbey BU/C 1
Bradwell BU/C 1
Brickhill, Gt BU/C 1 & BUF 7.1.2 Mfc
Brickhill Lt BU/C 1 & BUF 7.1.2 Mfc
Brill OX/C3
Broughton BU/C 1
Buckingham BUF 8.2.1 Mfc
Castlethorpe BU/C 1
Chalfont St Giles BU/C 1
Chalfont St Peter BU/C 1
Chalvey [Heritage Vol 2/2-3 BU/PER]
Chartridge BU/C 1
Chearsley BUF 5.1.2 Mfc
Chenies BU/C 1
Chesham BU/C 1
Chesham Bois BU/C 1
Chichley BU/C 1 & BUF 7.3.1 Mfc
Chilton OX/C 3
Cholesbury BUF 5.3 Mfc
Clifton Reynes BU/C 1&BUF 7.3.2 Mfc
Cold Brayfield BU/C 1 & BUF 7.3.2 Mfc
Coleshill BU/C 1
Crawley, North BU/C 1
Crendon, Long OX/C 3
Cublington BUF 5.4.1 Mfc
Cuddington BUF 5.1.2 Mfc
Dagnall BU/C 1

Dinton BUF 5.2.1 Mfc
Dorton OX/C 3
Edelsborough BU/C 1
Eton BUF 3.2.3 Mfc
Farnham Royal BU/C 1
Fawley OX/C 3
Fenny Stratford BU/C 1
Filgrave BU/C 1
Fleet Marston BUF 5.1.2
Gayhurst BU/C 1 & BUF 7.3.1.1b Mfc
Halton BUF 5.3 Mfc
Hambledon OX/C 2
Hanslope BU/C 1
Hardmead BU/C 1 & BUF 7.3.1 Mfc
Hardwick BUF 5.4.1 Mfc
Hartwell 5.2.1Mfc
Haversham BU/C 1
Hawridge BUF 5.3 Mfc
Hedgerley Dean BUF 3.1.1 Mfc
Hedgerley Fulmer BUF 3.1.1 Mfc
Hitcham BU/C 1 & BUF 3.3.3 Mfc
Hundridge BU/C 1
Ickford OX/C 3
Lacey Green BUF 7.3.1 Mfc
Lathbury BU/C 1 & BUF 7.3.1b Mfc
Latimer BU/C 1
Lavendon BU/C 1 & BUF 7.3.2 Mfc
Lee BU/C 1
Linford, Little BU/C 1
Linford, Great BU/C 1
Longwick BU/C 1 & shelf 9
Loughton BU/C 1
Marlow, Lt BUF 4.1.3 Mfc
Marlow, Gt BUF 4.2.1 Mfc
Milton Keynes BU/C 1
Missenden, Gt BU/C 1
Moulsoe BU/C 1
Newport Pagnell BU/C 1
Newton Blossomville BU/C 1
                        & BUF 7.3.2 Mfc
Newton Longville BU/C 1
Northall BU/C 1

Oakley OX/C 3
Olney with Warrington BU/C 1
Penn BU/C 1
Princes Risborough BUF 7.3.1a & shelf 9
Quarrendon BUF 5.1.2 Mfc
Ravenstone BU/C 1 & BUF 7.3.4
Seer Green BU/C 1
Shabbington OX/C 3
Shenley BU/C 1
Sherington BU/C 1 & BUF 7.3.1b Mfc
Simpson BU/C 1
Slapton BU/C 1
St. Leonards BUF 5.3 Mfc
Stantonbury BU/C 1
Stoke Goldington BUF 7.3.4 Mfc
Tyringham BU/C 1 & BUF 7.3.1 Mfc
Waddesdon BUF 5.1.2 Mfc

Walton BU/C 1
Warrington BU/C 1
Water Eaton BU/C 1
Waterside BU/C 1
Wavendon BU/C1
Weedon BUF 5.4.1Mfc
Westcott BUF 5.4.2 Mfc
Weston Underwood BU/C 1
 & BUF 7.3.4 Mfc
Weston Turville BUF 5.3 Mfc
Whitchurch NUF 5.4.1 Mfc
Willen BU/C 1
Winchendon, Lower 5.1.2 Mfc
Woodrow BU/C 1
Woolstone, Gt BU/C 1
Woughton on the Green BU/C 1
Wycombe, High BUF 4.1.2 Mfc

BUCKINGHAMSHIRE **1851 2% Sample** (see surname index) [Mfc]
  Beachampton; Dorney; Great Horwood

BUCKINGHAMSHIRE **1861**
  Bletchley [BU/C 1]
  Brickhill, Great [BU/C 1]
  Hitcham [BU/C 1]
  Simpson [BU/C 1]
  Water Eaton [BU/C 1]

Buckinghamshire FHS 1861 Census
REGISTRATION DISTRICT   **RG 9**   * = Microfilm held
Amersham RD *part* - Missenden & Chesham SDs   0844-0846*
Aylesbury RD *part* - Aston Clinton & Wadddesdon SDs   0867-0868*
Leighton Buzzard RD Bucks *part* -Eddlesborough SD   1009*

BUCKINGHAMSHIRE **1871**
  Bletchley [BU/C 1]
  Brickhill, Great [BU/C 1]
  Hitcham [BU/C 1]
  Quainton [BU/C 1]
  Water Eaton [BU/C 1]

BUCKINGHAMSHIRE **1881**
GSU Transcripts & Indexes -county complete [Lower Library Mfc]

BUCKINGHAMSHIRE **1891**
Buckinghamshire & Oxfordshire 1891Census Index - Oxfordshire FHS [OXT];
Buckinghamshire FHS 1891 Census Index [BUF]

REGISTRATION DISTRICT	**RG 12**	**Volume No**	**Location**
Newport Pagnell RD - Olney & Weston Underwood SD [ff4-187]	1152	BUF	Mfc
Wycombe RD - High Wycombe SD [ff64-141]	1139	BUF	Mfc
Henley RD - Buckinghamshire part	1156-1159	OXT	Mfc
Thame RD - Buckinghamshire part	1160-1161	OXT	Mfc

Oxfordshire FHS 1891 Census Index - Thame RD [OXT]; Oxfordshire FHS 1891 Census Index - Henley RD [OXH]; Buckinghamshire 1891 Census Indexes [BUF]

PARISH	Volume	Location	PARISH	Volume	Location
Aylesbury	BUF	Mfc	Linford, Little	BUF 7.3.2	Mfc
Brill	OXT	Mfc	Marlow, Little	BUF	Mfc
Crendon, Long	OXT	Mfc	Oakley	OXT	Mfc
Dorton	OXT	Mfc	Olney with Warrington	BUF 7.3.1	Mfc
Fawley	OXH	Mfc	Ravenstone	BUF 7.3.2	Mfc
Gayhurst	BUF 7.3.2	Mfc	Shabington	OXT	Mfc
Hambledon	OXH	Mfc	Stoke Goldington	BUF 7.3.2	Mfc & BU/C 1
Haversham	BUF 7.3.2	Mfc			
Hedsor	BUF	Mfc	Tyringham	BUF 7.3.2	Mfc
Ickford	OXT	Mfc	Weston Underwood	BUF 7.3.2	Mfc
Lathbury	BUF 7.3.2	Mfc	Wooburn	BUF	Mfc

CAMBRIDGESHIRE (CA)

1767 CA papist return (CRS Occ Paper 2) [RC/PER]
1811 Ely St Mary, (CAFHSJ 3/7) [CA/PER]

CAMBRIDGESHIRE **1841**
Censearch Index to its own unpublished transcript - county complete [Mfc]

CAMBRIDGESHIRE **1841**
Whaddon [SP 7/8]
Whittlesey [CA/C 23 & Mf 2648]

The 1841 districts were based upon the Hundreds.
The Society holds the following microfilms:

DISTRICT/HUNDRED	HO 107
Armingford, Chesterton, Cheveley	0063-0065
Chilford, Flendish	0066-0067
Papworth, Radfield, Staine	0070-0072
Staplow, Thriplow, Wetherley, Whittlesford	0073-0076
Witchford North (Isle of Ely)	0080-0082
Witchford South & Cambridge Borough	0083-0085

CAMBRIDESHIRE **1851**
Cambridgeshire RO & FHS 1851 Census Transcripts & Indexes
Master Name Index [CA/C 20] County Complete   * = Microfilm held

REGISTRATION DISTRICT	HO 107	Location
Cambridge RD	1760*	CA/C 18,19
Caxton RD	1758*	CA/C 9
Chesterton RD	1759*	CA/C 7,8,15
Ely RD	1764*	CA/C 1,3,12 or shelf 9
Linton RD	1761*	CA/C 5
Newmarket RD	1762-1763*	CA/C 11,16
North Witchford RD	1765*	CA/C 4,6
Whittlesey RD	1765*	CA/C 10 or Shelf 9 or Mf 2649
Wisbech RD	1766-1767*	CA/C 2 or Shelf 9
Peterborough RD - Cambridgeshire part	1747*	CA/C 4
Royston RD - Cambridgeshire part	1707-1708*	CA/C 14

St Ives RD - Cambrideshire part	1749*	CA/C 7
Welney RD - Cambridgeshire part	1830*	CA/C 12

CAMBRIDGESHIRE **1851** 2% Sample [Surname index]
Wendy; Great Wilbraham [Mfc]

CAMBRIDGESHIRE **1861**
REGISTRATION DISTRICT	RG 9		* = Microfilm held
Cambridge RD	1023-1027*		
Caxton RD	1016-1017*		
Chesterton RD	1018-1022*		
Ely RD	1037-1041*		
Linton RD	1028-1030*		
Newmarket RD	1031-1036*		
North Witchford RD	1042-1044*		
Whittlesey RD	1045-1046*		
Wisbech RD	1047-1053*		

CAMBRIDGESHIRE **1861**
Ashley cum Silverley [CA/C 25]   Newmarket [CA /C25]
Burwell [CA/C 25]   Snailwell [CA/C 23]
Kennett [CA/C 25]   Swaffham Prior [CA/C 25]
Landwade [CA/C 25]   Whittlesey [CA/C 23 & Mf 2850]

CAMBRIDGESHIRE **1871**
Cambridge FHS 1871 Census Index
REGISTRATION DISTRICT	RG 11	Location	* = Microfilm held
Cambridge Borough RD	1585-1590	CA/C 21-2	
Whittlesey RD		CA/C 24 & Mf 2851	

CAMBRIDGESHIRE **1881**
GSU Transcript & Indexes - county complete [Lower Library Mfc]

CHESHIRE (CH)

- **1705** CH papist return [RC/LST]
- **1767** CH papist return (CRS Occ Paper 1) [RC/PER]
- **1821** Newton by Chester census (CH Sheaf 3rd ser 13/3153); Rosthern cen (FHS CH 1/2-4) [*both* CH/PER]

CHESHIRE **1841-1881** Place Name Index [CH/C 3]

CHESHIRE **1841**
The 1841 districts were based upon the Hundreds.
All microfilms for the county are held as follows:
DISTRICT/HUNDRED	HO 107		
Broxton	89-90	Stockport	108-113
Bucklow	91-95	Nantwich	116-118
Eddisbury	96-98	Northwich	119-122
Macclesfield	100-107, 115, 132	Wirral	123-129
		Chester	130-131

CHESHIRE **1851**
FHS Cheshire 1851 Census Index Vols 1-12 [CHF] County complete.   * = Microfilm held

REGISTRATION DISTRICT	HO 107	Volume No.	Location
Altrincham RD	2162-2163*	CHF 5	CH/C 6 or 1
Congleton RD	2167-2168*	CHF 8	CH/C 7
Great Boughton RD	2171-2172*	CHF 10	CH/C 7
Macclesfield RD	2158-2161*	CHF 3-4	CH/C 6 or 1 & 5
Nantwich RD	2169-2170*	CHF 9	CH/C 7
Northwich RD	2165-2166*	CHF 7	CH/C 7
Northwich RD	2165*		CH/C 2
Runcorn RD	2164*	CHF 6	CH/C 6
Stockport RD	2154-2157*	CHF 1-2	CH/C 2 or 6
Wirral RD	2173-2175	CHF 11-12	CH/C 7

CHESHIRE **1861** County complete   * = Microfilm held

REGISTRATION DISTRICT	RG9	REGISTRATION DISTRICT	RG9
Altrincham RD	2588-2594*	Nantwich RD	2615-2623*
Birkenhead RD	2639-1649*	Northwich RD	2600-2607*
Congleton RD	2608-2614*	Runcorn RD	2595-2599*
Great Boughton RD	2171-2172*	Stockport RD	2556-2572*
Macclesfield RD	2574-2587*	Wirrall RD	2635-2638*

CHESHIRE **1881**
GSU Transcript & Indexes - county complete [Lower Library Mfc]

FHS Cheshire 1881 Census Indexes [CFH]
REGISTRATION DISTRICT	RG 11	Volume No.	Location
Altrincham RD	3502-3507	CFH	Mfc

CHESHIRE **1891**
FHS Cheshire 1891 Census Indexes [CFH]
REGISTRATION DISTRICT	RG 12	Volume No.	Location
Congleton RD	2843-2848	CFH	Mfc
Macclesfield RD	2808-2819	CFH	Mfc
Northwich RD	2835-2842	CFH	CH/C 8
Runcorn RD - Frodsham SD	2843	CFH	Mfc
Stockport RD	2788-2807	CFH	CH/C 8

CORNWALL (CO)

1649-50   Cornwall Duchy parliamentary survey (*in 2 pts*) (Devon & Cornwall Record Society new series 25 & 27) [DE/PER]
1767   CO papist return (CRS Occ Paper 2) [RC/PER]
1821   Veryan census [CO/C 19]

CORNWALL **1841**
The 1841 districts were based on the Hundreds.
The Society holds microfilms for the following Hundreds:
DISTRICT/HUNDRED   HO 107
Penwith *part* & Powder *part*   156

CORNWALL 1851
New Zealand Gen Soc - Cornish Group 1851 Census Index [NZC] and Ray Woodbine's
Transcripts & Indexes [RW]. * = Microfilm held

REGISTRATION DISTRICT	HO 107	Volume No.	Location
Bodmin RD	1904*	NZC 10-11 or RW 4	CO/C 1 or C 7
Camelford RD	1898*	NZC 4	CO/C 1
Falmouth RD			
- Mylor SD *part 1*	1911*	NZC 22	CO/C 2B
- Mylor part 2 & Constantine SDs	1911*	NZC 23	CO/C 2B
Helston RD	1912-1913*	NZC 31-33	CO/C 2C
- Wendron SD	1912*	NZC 31	CO/C 2C
- Helston SD	1912*	NZC 32	CO/C 2C
- St Keverne SD	1913*	NZC 32	CO/C 2C
- Breage SD	1913*	NZC 33	CO/C 2C
- Crowan SD	1913*	NZC 33	CO/C 2C
Helston RD *(part)* Lizzard parishes	1912-1913*		Mfc (shelf 9)
Launceston RD	1899*	NZC 6-7	CO/C 1
Liskeard RD			
- Callington SD	1901*	NXC 3 or RW 1	CO/C 1 or C 4
- Liskeard SD	1902*	NZC 2 & 3 or RW 2	CO/C 1 or C 5
- Looe SD	1903*	NZC 1 or RW 3	CO/C 1 or C 6
Penzance RD			
- Uny Lelant SD	1917*	NZC 24	CO/C 2B
- St Ives SD	1917*	NZC 25	CO/C 2B
- Marazion SD	1918*	NZC 26	CO/C 2B
- Penzance SD	1918*	NZC 27-28	CO/C 2B
- St Just in Penwith SD	1919*		
- St Buryan SD	1919*		
Redruth RD	1914-1916*	NZC 34-38	CO/C 2C
- Gwennup SD	1914*	NZC 34	CO/C 2C
- Redruth SD	1915*	NZC 35	CO/C 2C
- Illogan SD	1915*	NZC 36	CO/C 2C
- Camborne & Phillack SDs	1916*	NZC 37-8	CO/C 2C
Scilly Isles RD	1919*		
St Austell RD			
- Fowey SD	1906*	RW 6	CO/C 10
- St Austell SD	1907*	NZC 15	CO/C 2A
- Mevagissey/Grampound SDs	1908*	NZC 16	CO/C 2A
St Columb RD	1905*	NZC 12-13 or RW 5	CO/C 2 or C 9
- Padstow SD	1905*	NZC 12	CO/C 2A
- St Columb SD	1905*	NZC 13	CO/C 2A
- Newlyn SD	1905*	NZC 13	CO/C 2A
St Germans RD	1900*	NZC 8-9	CO/C 1
Stratton RD	1897*	NZC 5	CO/C 1
Truro RD			
- Probus/St Just & St Agnes SDs	1909*	NZC 17-18	CO/C 2A
- St Clement/Kenwyn & Kea SDs	1910*	NZC 19-21	CO/C 2A

* = Microfilm held

CORNWALL 1861

REGISTRATION DISTRICT	RG 9
Camelford RD	1515-1516*
Launceston RD - Alterton SD	1517*

Penzance RD - Penzance *part*/ St Just in
Penwith & St Buryan SDs   1593-1599*
Scilly Isles RD   1600*
Stratton RD   1512-1514*

CORNWALL **1881**
GSU Transcript & Indexes - county complete [Lower Library Mfc]

CUMBERLAND (CU)

1762 Whitehaven [CU/C 1]
1765 Maryport [CU/C 1]
1767 CU papist return (*in 2 vols*) (CRS Occ Papers 1 & 2) [RC/PER]; Copeland Deanery papist return (CU FHS N/L 36) [CU/PER]
1792 Maryport [CU/C 1]
c1800 Maryport [CU/C 1]

CUMBERLAND **1841**
The 1841 districts were based upon the Hundreds.
The Society holds microfilms for the following:
DISTRICT/HUNDRED   HO 107
Allerdale above Derwent   156-158

CUMBERLAND **1851 2% Sample** [see surname index] [Mfc]
Brampton; Cockermouth; Glassonbury; Hawksdale; Lamplugh; Lyneside; Nenthead; Wythop

CUMBERLAND **1851**
Cumbria FHS 1851 Census Indexes
Guide to Enumeration Districts & Place Name Index [CU/C 7]

REGISTRATION DISTRICT	HO 107		Location
Alston RD	2424		CU/C 4
Bootle RD	2438		CU/C 1 or 8
Brampton RD	2427		
Carlisle RD			
- Wetheral & St Cuthbert SDs	2429	[ff 5-246, 251-551]	CU/C 5 & 4
- Carlisle St Mary SD pts 1-5	2430	[ff 5-477]	CU/C 5
- Stanwix, Burgh & Dalston SDs	2431		
Cockermouth RD	2434	[ff 330-507]	CU/C 6
Cockermouth RD	2435	[ff 92-206]	CU/C 6
Longtown RD	2428		
Penrith RD			
- Penrith SD	2425		CU/C 4
- Greystoke/Kirkoswald SDs	2426		CU/C 4
Whitehaven RD			
- Harrington/Whitehaven SDs	2436		CU/C 9
- Whitehaven/St Bees SDs	2437		CU/C 8
Wigton RD			
- Wigton SD *part*	2432		CU/C 10
- Abbeyholme/Coldbeck SDs	2433		CU/C 10

CUMBERLAND **1881**
GSU Transcript & Indexes - county complete [Lower Library Mfc]

DERBYSHIRE (DB)

1767 DB papist return (CRS Occ Paper 2) [RC/PER]
1778 Morley census (Branch News 50) [DB/PER]
1787 Morley census (Branch News 51) [DB/PER]
1801 Smalley [DB/L 19]
1811 Littleover & Mickleover census [DB/R 23]

DERBYSHIRE 1841
Derbyshire FHS journal [DBF]
PARISH INDEXES
Ashbourne Workhouse [DB/C 2]   Dethick (DBF/25) [DB/PER]
Chaddesden [DB/C 1]   Lea (DBF/25) [DB/PER]

DERBYSHIRE 1841
The 1841 districts were based upon the Hundreds.
The Society holds microfilms for the following districts:

DISTRICT/HUNDRED	HO 107
Morlestone/Litchurch	194
Scarsdale	194, 196
Wirksworth	197-198
Derby	199

DERBYSHIRE 1851
Derbyshire FHS 1851 Census Index [DBF]   * = Microfilm held

REGISTRATION DISTRICT	HO 107	Volume	Location
Ashbourne RD			
- Brailsford, Mayfield & Ashbourne SDs	2146	DBF 1.1	DB/C 2
- Calton, Hartington & Brassingham SDs	2146	DBF 1.2	DB/C 2
Ashby de la Zouch RD - Derbyshire part	2084*		
Bakewell RD			
- Bakewell SD	2149		
- Matlock SD	2150	DBF 3.2	DB/C 2
- Derbyshire part	2125-2126*		
- Tideswell SD	2150	DBF 3.3	DB/C 2
Belper RD			
- Duffield SD	2144	DBF 5.1	DB/C 2
- Horsley SD	2144	DBF 5.2	DB/C 2
- Belper SD	2144	DBF 5.3	DB/C 2
- Ripley SD	2145		
- Ripley & Alfreston SDs	2145		
- Wirksworth SD	2145	DBF 5.6	DB/C 2
Burton on Trent RD - Derbyshire part	2011*	DBF 6.1-2	DB/C 3
Chapel en le Frith RD	2155		
Chesterfield RD			
- Ashover SD	2147		
- Chesterfield SD	2147	DBF 8.2	DB/C 3
- Bolsover & Dronfield SDs	2148		
- Eckington SD	2148	DBF 8.4	DB/C 3
Derby RD			
- St Alkmund SD	2142*	DBF 9.1	DB/C 3
- St Peter SD	2143	DBF 9.2	DB/C 3
- St Peter SD (St Werburgh parish)	2143	DBF 9.3	DB/C 3

Ecclesall Bierlow RD - Derbyshire part	2336		
Hayfield RD			
- Glossop SD	2152	DBF 11.1	DB/C 3
- Hayfield SD	2153		
Mansfield RD - Derbyshire part	2123*	DBF 12.1	DB/C 3A
Rotherham RD - Derbyshire part	2434		
Shardlow RD			
- Melbourne SD	2140	DBF 14.1	DB/C 3A
- Shardlow SD	2140	DBF 14.2	DB/C 3A
- Stapleford SD	2141	DBF 14.3	DB/C 3A
- Spondon SD	2141*	DBF 14.4	DB/C 3A
Tamworth & Uttoxeter RDs - Derbyshire parts	2013*, 2010*	DBF 13.1	DB/C 3A
Worksworth RD - Derbyshire part	2122	DBF 12.1	DB/C 3A

DERBYSHIRE 1851 2% Sample [Surname Index] [Mfc]
  Ballidon; Brushfield; Coombs Edge; Hulland Ward (intakes); Littleover; Shipley

DERBYSHIRE 1861
REGISTRATION DISTRICT	RG 9	* = Microfilm held
Bakewell RD *part*	2539-2544*	
Chapel en le Frith RD	2545-2548*	
Hayfield RD	2549-2555*	

Nottinghamshire FHS 1861 Census Index [NTF] - Derbyshire parts
REGISTRATION DISTRICT	RG 9	Volume	Location
Basford RD - Derbyshire part	2442-2446	NTF 55	NT/C 5
Mansfield RD - Derbyshire part	2423-2430	NTF 46	NT/C 5
Worksop RD - Derbyshire part	2418-2422	NTF 41	NT/C 5

PARISHES COVERED:
Nottinghamshire FHS 1861 Census Index [NTF]; Derbyshire FHS Journal [DBF]
Astwith	NTF 46	NT/C 5
Ault Hucknall	NTF 46	NT/C 5
Barlborough	NTF 41	NTC/ 5
Blackwell	NTF 46	NT/C 5
Brassington House of Industry	DBF24	DB/PER
Chaddesden		DB/C 1
Clowne	NTF 41	NT/C 5
Codnor	NTF 55	NT/C 5
Codnor Park	NTF 55	NT/C 5
Elmton	NTF 41	NT/C 5
Glapwell	NTF 46	NT/C 5
Hardstoft	NTF 46	NT/C 5
Heanor	NTF 55	NT/C 5
Ilkeston	NTF 55	NT/C 5
Langwith, Upper	NTF 46	NT/C 5
Loscoe	NTF 55	NT/C 5
Normanton, South	NTF 46	NT/C 5
Palterton	NTF 46	NT/C 5
Pinxton	NTF 46	NT/C 5
Pleasley	NTF 46	NT/C 5
Pleasley Hill	NTF 46	NT/C 5
Scarcliffe	NTF 46	NT/C 5
Shipley	NTF 55	NT/C 5
Shirebrook	NTF 46	NT/C 5

Stainsby	NTF 46	NT/C 5
Stoneyford	NTF 55	NT/C 5
Stoney Houghton	NTF 46	NT/C 5
Tibshelf	NTF 46	NT/C 5
Whitwell	NTF 41	NT/C 5
Wood Lincoln	NTF 55	NT/C 5

DERBYSHIRE **1871**
Nottinghamshire FHS 1871 Census Index [NTF] - Derbyshire parts

REGISTRATION DISTRICT	RG 10	Volume	Location
Basford RD - Derbyshire part	3487-3498	NTF 71	NT/C 7
Mansfield RD - Derbyshire part	3464-3475	NTF 76	NT/C 7
Worksop RD - Derbyshire part	3458-3463	NTF 68	NT/C 7

PARISHES COVERED:
Notts FHS 1871Census Index [NTF]; Sheffield FHS journal [YSF].
A list of the Derbyshire parishes covered is in NTF 80 [NT/C 7]

Astwith	NTF 76	NT/C 7	Langwith, Upper	NTF 68	NT/C 7
Ault Hucknall	NTF 76	NT/C 7	Loscoe	NTF 71	NT/C 7
Barlborough	NTF 68	NTC/ 7	Marlpool	NTF 71	NT/C 7
Blackwell	NTF 76	NT/C 7	Normanton, South	NTF 76	NT/C 7
Chaddesden		DB/C 1	Palterton	NTF 76	NT/C 7
Chesterton Workhouse	YSF 7/2	YK/PER	Pinxton	NTF 76	NT/C 7
Clowne	NTF 68	NT/C 7	Pleasley	NTF 76	NT/C 7
Codnor	NTF 71	NT/C 7	Pleasley Hill	NTF 76	NT/C 7
Codnor Park	NTF 71	NT/C 7	Scarcliffe	NTF 76	NT/C 7
Creswell	NTF 68	NT/C 7	Shipley	NTF 71	NT/C 7
Elmton	NTF 68	NT/C 7	Shirebrook	NTF 76	NT/C 7
Glapwell	NTF 76	NT/C 7	Stainsby	NTF 76	NT/C 7
Hardstoft	NTF 76	NT/C 7	Stoneyford	NTF 71	NT/C 7
Heanor	NTF 71	NT/C 7	Stoney Houghton	NTF 76	NT/C 7
Ilkeston	NTF 71	NT/C 7	Tibshelf	NTF 76	NT/C 7
Langley	NTF 71	NT/C 7	Whitwell	NTF 68	NT/C 7
Langley Mill	NTF 71	NT/C 7			

DERBYSHIRE **1881**
GSU Transcript & Indexes - county complete [Lower Library Mfc]

DERBYSHIRE **1891**
Nottinghamshire FHS 1891 Census Index - Derbyshire parts [NTF];
Derbyshire FHS 1891 Census Index [DBF]

REGISTRATION DISTRICT	RG 12	Volume	Location
Asbourn RD - Hartington SD	2755	DBF	Mfc
Bakefield RD - Tideswell SD	2777	DBF	Mfc
Chesterfield RD - Chesterfield SD	2761	DBF	Mfc
Derby RD - Derby SD (St Werburgh)	2732	DBF	Mfc
Basford RD - Derbyshire part	2658-2670	NTF 85/4	NT/C 9
Burton on Trent RD - Derbyshire part	2197	DBF	Mfc
Mansfield RD - Derbyshire part	2648-2657	NTF 85/7	NT/C 9
Mansfield RD - Derbyshire part	2649	DBF	Mfc
Uttoxeter RD - Derbyshire part	2195	DBF	Mfc
Worksop RD - Derbyshire part	2643-2647	NTF 85/6	NT/C 9

PARISHES COVERED:
Notts FHS 1891 Census Index [NTF]; Derbyshire FHS 1891 Census Index [DBF]

Alsop Dale	DBF(2755)	Mfc	Langley Mill	NTF 85/4	NT/C 9
Astwith	NTF 85/7	NT/C 9	Langwith, Upper	NTF 85/7	NT/C 9
Ault Hucknall	DBF(2649)	Mfc	Langwith, Upper	DBF(2649)	Mfc
Ault Hucknall	NTF 85/7	NT/C 9	Loscoe	NTF 85/4	NT/C 9
Barlborough	NTF 85/6	NTC/ 9	Marston	DBF(2195)	Mfc
Blackwell	NTF 85/7	NT/C 9	Mickleover	DBF(2197)	Mfc
Boylestone	DBF(2195)	Mfc	Montgomery	DBF(2195)	Mfc
Bretby	DBF(2197)	Mfc	Newton	NTF 85/7	NT/C 9
Bulliden	DBF(2755)	Mfc	Newton Grange	DBF(2755)	Mfc
Chesterfield	DBF(2755)	Mfc	Normanton, South	NTF 85/7	NT/C 9
Clowne	NTF 85/6	NT/C 9	Palterton	NTF 85/7	NT/C 9
Codnor	NTF 85/4	NT/C 9	Parwich	DBF(2755)	Mfc
Codnor Park	NTF 85/4	NT/C 9	Pinxton	NTF 85/7	NT/C 9
Cotmanhay	NTF 85/4	NT/C 9	Plasley	DBF(2649)	Mfc
Cubley	DBF(2195)	Mfc	Pleasley Hill	NTF 85/7	NT/C 9
Derby St Werburgh	DBF(2732)	Mfc	Pleasley	NTF 85/7	NT/C 9
Doe Lea	NTF 85/7	NT/C 9	Repton	DBF(2197)	Mfc
Doveridge	DBF(2195)	Mfc	Riley	NTF 85/7	NT/C 9
Eaton	DBF(2755)	Mfc	Rowthorne	NTF 85/7	NT/C 9
Elmton	NTF 85/6	NT/C 9	Scarcliffe	DBF(2649)	Mfc
Eyam	DBF(2777)	Mfc	Scarcliffe	NTF 85/7	NT/C 9
Finder	DBF(2197)	Mfc	Shipley	NTF 85/4	NT/C 9
Glapwell	NTF 85/7	NT/C 9	Shirebrook	NTF 85/7	NT/C 9
Glapwell	DBF(2649)	Mfc	Somersal	DBF(2195)	Mfc
Hardstoft	NTF 85/7	NT/C 9	Stoney Houghton	NTF 85/7	NT/C 9
Hardwick	NTF 85/7	NT/C 9	Stoneyford	NTF 85/4	NT/C 9
Hartington	DBF(2755)	Mfc	Sudbury	DBF(2195)	Mfc
Heanor	NTF 85/4	NT/C 9	Tibshelf	NTF 85/7	NT/C 9
Herbert	DBF(2195)	Mfc	Whitwell	NTF 85/6	NT/C 9
Ilkeston	NTF 85/4	NT/C 9	Willington	DBF(2197)	Mfc

DEVON (DE)

1649-50 Cornwall Duchy parliamentary survey (DE & CO Rec Soc new ser 27) [DE/PER]
1767 DE papist return (CRS Occ Paper 2) [RC/PER]
late 18C Pilton: Pulchras manor roll extracts [DE/L 68]
1790 Sandford (DE FHn 53) [DE/PER]
1793 Sandford (DE FHn 53) [DE/PER]
1800 Sandford (DE FHn 53) [DE/PER]

DEVON **1841**
The 1841 districts were based upon the Hundreds. The Society holds the following microfilms:

DISTRICT/HUNDRED	HO 107
Axminster/Bampton/Braunton	201-203
Coleridge/Colyton	211-214
Plymouth Pt	269-270

DEVON **1851**
GSU 1851 Transcript & Indexes - county complete [Mfc]

DEVON **1851**
Devonshire FHS 1851 Census Index Vols 1-39. Includes Master Place Index [DEF]
County Complete.   * = Microfilm held

REGISTRATION DISTRICT	HO 107	Volume	Location
Axminster RD	1862*	DEF 11	DE/C 4
Barnstable RD	1892-1893*	DEF 3, 15	DE/C 4
- Barnstable, Paracombe & Combmartin SDs	1892*	DEF 3	DE/C 4
- Ilfracombe, Braunceston & Bishops Tawton SDs	1893*	DEF 15	DE/C 4
Bideford RD	1895*	DEF 2	DE/C 4
Crediton RD	1886-1887*	DEF 33, 32	DE/C 6
- Morchard Bishop SD	1886*	DEF 33	DE/C 6
- Crediton & Cheriton Fitzpaine SDs	1887*	DEF 32	DE/C 6
East Stonehouse RD	1880*	DEF 4	DE/C 4
Exeter RD			
- St Sidwell SD	1868*	DEF 16	DE/C 5
- St David SD	1869*	DEF 12	DE/C 5
Holsworthy RD	1896*	DEF 18	DE/C 5
Honiton RD	1863-1864*	DEF 11, 9	DE/C 4
Kingsbridge RD	1875*	DEF 30	DE/C 6
Kingsbridge RD	1876*	DEF 13	DE/C 5
Newton Abbot RD	1870-1872*	DEF 33,22,38	DE/C 6 & 5
- Teignmouth & Chudleigh SDs	1870*	DEF 33	DE/C 6
- Moreton Hampstead, Ashburton & Newton Abbot SDs	1871*	DEF 22	DE/C 5
- Torquay SD	1872*	DEF 38	DE/C 6
Okehampton RD	1885*	DEF 26	DE/C 5
Plymouth RD	1878-1879*	DEF 6, 5	DE/C 4
Plympton St Mary RD	1877*	DEF 17	DE/C 5
South Molton RD	1891*	DEF 1	DE/C 4
St Thomas RD	1865-1867*	DEF 23, 25,21	DE/C 5
- East Buckleigh, Exmouth & Woodhay SDs	1865*	DEF 23	DE/C 5
- Broad Clist, Topsham & Heavitree SDs	1866*	DEF 25	DE/C 5
- Alphington & Christow SDs	1867*	DEF 21	DE/C 5
Stoke Damerel RD	1881-1882*	DEF 7, 8	DE/C 4
Tavistock RD	1883-1884*	DEF 19, 20	DE/C 5
Tiverton RD	1888-1890*	DEF 31,24, 27	DE/C 5 & 6
- Silverton, Cullompton & Uffculme SDs	1888*	DEF 31	DE/C 6
- Tiverton & Washfield SDs	1889*	DEF 27	DE/C 6
- Bampton & Dulverton SDs	1890*	DEF 24	DE/C 5
Torrington RD	1894*	DEF 14	DE/C 5
Totnes RD	1873-1874*	DEF 29, 28	DE/C 6
Chard RD - Devon part	1927	DEF 36	DE/C 6
Launceston RD - Devon part	1899*	DEF 37	DE/C 6
Taunton RD - Devon part	1922	DEF 35	DE/C 6
Wellington RD - Devon part	1921	DEF 39	DE/C 6

DEVON 1861 County complete   * = Microfilm held
REGISTRATION DISTRICT   RG 9   REGISTRATION DISTRICT   RG 9
Axminster RD   1370-1374*   Plymouth RD   1434-1445*
Barnstable RD   1488-1496*   Plympton St Mary RD   1427-1433*
Cediton RD   1470-1475*   South Molton RD   1483-1487*
East Stonehouse RD   1446-1447*   St Thomas RD   1381-1392*
Exeter RD   1393-1399*   Stoke Damerel RD   1448-1456*
Holsworthy RD   1507-1511*   Tavistock RD   1457-1464*
Honiton RD   1375-1380*   Tiverton RD   1476-1482*
Kingsbridge RD   1422-1426*   Torrington RD   1497-1482*
Newton Abbot RD   1400-1413*   Totnes RD   1414-1421*
Okehampton RD   1465-1469*

DEVON 1881
GSU Transcript & Indexes - county complete [Lower Library Mfc]

DEVON 1891
Devon FHS 1891 North Devon Census Index [DEF]

REGISTRATION DISTRICT	RG 12	Location
Barnstable RD		
- Combe Martin SD	1776	Mfc
- Parracombe SD	1775	Mfc
- Bishops Tawton SD	1780	Mfc
- Ilfracombe SD	1777-1779	Mfc
- Barnstable SD	1773-1774	Mfc
Bideford RD		
- Northam SD	1787	Mfc
- Parkham SD	1788	Mfc
- Bideford SD	1786	Mfc
- Bradworthy SD	1790	Mfc
- Hartland SD	1789	Mfc
Crediton RD		
- Morchard Bishop SD	1758	Mfc
- Bow SD	1759	Mfc
Holsworthy RD		
- Black Torrington SD	1793	Mfc
- Broadwoodwidger SD	1794	Mfc
- Holsworthy SD	1792	Mfc
- Clawton SD	1795	Mfc
- Milton Dameral SD	1791	Mfc
South Molton RD		
- Witheridge SD	1769	Mfc
- Exmoor SD	1770	Mfc
- South Molton SD	1771-1772	Mfc
Torrington RD		
- Great Torrington SD	1785	Mfc
- Dolton SD	1783	Mfc
- High Bickington RD	1781	Mfc
- Shebbear SD	1784	Mfc
- Winkleigh SD	1782	Mfc

DORSET (DO)

1724-29 Puddletown (DO Rec Soc 11) [DO/PER]
1767 DO papist return (CRS Occ Paper 2) [RC/PER]
1769 Puddletown (DO Rec Soc 11) [DO/PER]
1790 Corfe Castle (J DO FHS 3/1) [DO/PER] & [DO/C 7]
1801 Oborne (SO & DO N&Q 15/115) [SO/PER]

DORSET 1841
1841 districts were based upon the Hundreds.
The Society holds microfilms of the following Hundreds:
DISTRICT/HUNDRED   HO 107
Blandford North Division - Coombes Ditch,
  Pimperne & Rushmore, Dewlish Liberty   0277
Blandford - South Division - Corfe Castle, Bere Regis
Hundredsbarrow, Hasilor, Rowbarrow, Winfrith
  & Bindon & Owermoigne Liberties   0278
Shaston East Division (part) -Badbury, Cogden
  Cranborne, Loosebarrow & Monkton up Wimborne   0287

DORSET 1851
Somerset & Dorset FHS - Dorset 1851 Census Index Vols 1-14, includes Master Surname & Place Index [DOF]. GSU pilot project 1851 census transcript & indexes of **Devon** including cross county districts [GSD]
County Complete   * = Microfilm held

REGISTRATION DISTRICT	HO 107	Volume	Location
Beaminster RD	1860*	DOF 14	DO/C 5
Blandford RD	1853*	DOF 9, 12	DO/C 4
Bridport RD	1861*	DOF 6, 14	DO/C 3 & 4 or 6
Dorchester RD	1858	DOF 3, 4	DO/C 2
Poole RD	1853	DOF 5	DO/C 3
Shaftsbury RD	1851*	DOF 10, 11	DO/C 4 or 6
Sherborne RD	1859*	DOF 8	DO/C 3
Sturminster RD	1852*	DOF 10	DO/C 4
Wareham RD	1856	DOF 7, 8	DO/C 3
Weymouth RD	1857*	DOF 1, 2	DO/C 2 or 6
Wimborne RD	1854*	DOF 12, 13	DO/C 4 & 5
Axminster RD - Dorset part	1862*	DOF 14 & GSD	DO/C 5
Mere RD - Dorset part	1850	DOF 11	DO/C 4 or 6

DORSET 1851 2% Sample [surname index] [Mfc]
  Goathill; Iwerne Courtney; Kingston Russell; Shittenton; Stour East

DORSET 1861   * = Microfilm held

REGISTRATION DISTRICT	RG 9	REGISTRATION DISTRICT	RG 9
Beaminster RD	1362-1365*	Sherborne RD	1359-1361*
Blandford RD	1331-1334*	Sturminster RD	1329-1330*
Bridport RD	1366-1369*	Wareham RD	1343-1347*
Dorchester RD	1353-1358*	Weymouth RD	1348-1352*
Poole RD	1339-1342*	Wimborne RD	1335-1338*
Shaftsbury RD	1325-1328*		

DORSET **1881**
GSU Transcript & Indexes - county complete   [Lower Library Mfc]

DORSET **1891**
Somerset & Dorset FHS 1891 Census Index [DOF]
REGISTRATION DISTRICT	RG 12	Volume	Location
Shaftsbury RD			
-Shaftsbury, Cann & Motcombe SD	1628	DOF 1	DO/C 8
Cranbourne RD - Cranbourne SD	1635	DOF 2	DO/C 8
Wimborne RD - Wimbourne SD	1636	DOF 3	DO/C 8
Weymouth RD - Weymouth SD	1646-1647	DOF 4	DO/C 8

DURHAM (DU)

1647 Durham Diocese parliamentary survey (*in 2 vols*) (Surtees Soc 183 & 185) [DU/PER]
1767 DU papist return (CRS Occ Paper 2) [RC/PER]

DURHAM **1851**
Northumberland & Durham FHS - Durham 1851 Census Index [DNF];
Cleveland FHS 1851 Census Indexes [CYF]   * = Microfilm held

REGISTRATION DISTRICT	HO 107	Volume	Location
Auckland RD	2385-2386		
- Hutton Henry, Castle Eden	2385	CYF 45-46	YK/C 17
- Bishop Auckland	2385	CYF 79	YK/C 24
- Byers Green, Hunwick & Helmington, Newton Gap, Pollards Lands	2385	CYF 80	YK/C 24
- Auckland St Andrew	2385	CYF 82	YK/C 25
- Coundon	2385	CYF 83	YK/C 25
- Shildon	2385	CYF 111	YK/C 27
- Auckland St Helen, Middridge, Helmington Row, Crook	2385	CYF 113	YK/C 27
- Escombe, Coundon Grange	2385	CYF 114	YK/C 27
- Eldon, Windlestone, E.Thickley	2385	CYF 115	YK/C 27
- Old Park, Whitworth (ff 42-60)	2385		DU/C 9
Chester Le Street RD	2394		DU/C 8
Darlington RD	2382		
- Darlington St John, Darlington St Cuthbert, Darlington Holy Trinity	2382	CYF 41 a-c	YK/C 17
- Mancliffe, Cliffe, Cleasby, Stapleton, Blackwell, Barton, Oxneyfield & Newton Morrell	2382	CYF 48	YK/C 17
- Killerby, Walworth, School Aycliffe, Coatshaw Moor, Redworth, Great Aycliffe, Brafferton	2382	CYF 49	YK/C 17
- Neasham, Middleton St George & Middleton One Row (inc Goosepool & Oak Tree), Hurworth	2382	CYF 50	YK/C 17
- Heighington, Barmpton, Whessoe, Coatham Mundeville, Haughton le Skerne, Morton Palms, Sadberge & Great Burdon	2382	CYF 53	YK/C 18
- Consiscliffe, Carlbury, Piercebridge, Cockerton, Ardchdeacon Newton, Coldsides, Houghton le Side, Denton, Summerhouses	2382	CYF 69	YK/C 19
Durham RD	2389-2391		
- Lanchester SD (ff176-651)	2389		DU/C 2

- City *part* (ff 110-419) 2390 DU/C 7
- Tudhoe (ff 73-83) 2390 DU/C 9
- City *part* (ff 1-190) 2391 DU/C 7
Easington RD 2392
Gateshead RD 2401-2403
- Heworth SD 2401 DNF 4 DU/C 8
- Gateshead & Whickham SDs 2402-2403 DNF 7, 9 Mfc
Houghton Le Spring RD 2393 DNF 8 Mfc
South Shields RD 2399-2400 DNF 1-2 DU/C8&4
- Westoe SD 2399*
Stockton RD 2383-2384
- Long Newton & Elton, 2383 CYF 1 YK/C 1
 Redmarshall (*part*), Egglescliffe (inc Aislaby
 & Newsham), Grindon (inc Whitton)
- High & Low Worsall, Kirklevington 2383 CYF 2 YK/C 1
 & Picton, Stainton (inc Maltby &
 Ingleby Barwick), Acklam, Linthorpe (inc Ayresome & Newport)
- Yarm & Thornaby 2383 CYF 3-4 YK/C 1
- Stockton SD (inc Hartburn & Preston) 2383 CYF 12 a&b YK/C 1
- Middlesborough SD 2383 CYF 14 a&b YK/C 2
- Norton 2383 CYF 16 YK/C 2
- Billingham, Claxton, Cowpen 2384 CYF 11 YK/C 2
 Bewley, Greatham, Haverton Hill,
 Newton Bewley, Port Clarence, Wolviston
- Hartlepool SD 2384 CYF 17 a&b YK/C 2
- Stranton (*later West Hartlepool*) 2384 CYF 20 YK/C 2
- Hart, Thorp Bulmer, Elwick, Throston,
 Dalton Piercy, Brierton, Elwick Hall,
 Seaton Carew 2384 CYF 22 YK/C 3
- Trimdon, Butterwick, Embleton,
 Fishburn 2384 CYF 30 YK/C 10
- Bishopton, Great & Little Stainton,
 Elstob & Preston le Skerne, E. & W. Newbiggin,
 Bishop Middleham, Garmondsway &
 Thrislington, Mainsworth 2384 CYF 32 YK/C 11
- Cornforth & Great Chilton 2384 CYF 33 YK/C 11
- Ferryhill & Sedgefield 2384 CYF 43-44 YK/C 17
Sunderland RD 2395-2398
- Bishopwearmouth SD 2395 DNF 5-6 Mfc
- Sunderland 2396-2398
Teesdale RD 2387
- Middleton in Teesdale 2387 CYF 51 YK/C 18
- Barnard Castle 2387 CYF 52 a&b YK/C 18
- Staindrop & Walkerfield 2387 CYF 58 YK/C 18
- Cockfield, Woodland, Langley Dale
 & Shotton, Raby & Keverstone 2387 CYF 60 YK/C 18
- Hilton, Morton Tinmouth, Ingleton,
 Headlam, Langton, Gainford 2387 CYF 61 YK/C 19
- Cleatham, Winston with Newsham,
 Barforth, Ovington, Wycliffe, Hutton Magna,
 Barningham, Scargill, Hope 2387 CYF 66 YK/C 19
- Brignall, Rokeby, Boldron, Bowes,
 Streatlam, Stainton, Marwood 2387 CYF 73 YK/C 24
- Gilmonby, Whorlton, Westwick,
 Egglestone Abbey, Startforth 2387 CYF 74 YK/C 24

- Eggleston, Newbiggin with Bowlees, Forest & Frith with Harwood	2387	CYF 75	YK/C 24
- Lartington, Cotherstone, Hunderthwaite, Romaldkirk Mickleton, Lundale, Holwick	2387	CYF 84a-b	YK/C 25
Weardale RD	2388		
- St Johns Chapel	2388	CYF 76	YK/C
- Stanhope SD	2388	DNF 10	Mfc

DURHAM 1861

REGISTRATION DISTRICT	RG 9	
Auckland RD	3705-3716*	* = Microfilm held
Darlington RD part	3679-3683*	
Easington RD part	3746-3750*	
Hartlepool RD	3699-3704*	
Stockton RD part	3690-3698*	
Teesdale RD	3717-3722*	
Weardale RD part	3723-3726*	

DURHAM 1881
GSU Transcript & Indexes - county complete [Lower Library Mfc]

DURHAM 1891

REGISTRATION DISTRICT	RG 12	Volume	Location
Darlington RD			
- Darlington & Darlington North	4042	CYF	Mfc
Lanchester RD - Consett SD	4089-4090	CYF	Mfc

ESSEX (ES)

1767 ES papist return (CRS Occ Paper 2) [RC/PER]
1796 Ardleigh census [ES/L 71]

ESSEX **Pre 1841** census listings - Essex FHS microfiche Series no 2 [Mfc Shelf 9]

Adshdon	1810			Ingatestone	1831		
Ardleigh	1811	1821		Kelvedon	1830		
Ashdon	1801			Leyton	1821	1831	
Baddow, Little	1801	1821	1831	Middleton	1811	1815	
Beaumont cum Moze	1821			Mistley	1821		
Bentley, Little	1831			Mundon	1831		
Bradwell on Sea	1811			Norton Mandeville	1801		
Braintree	1821			Parndon, Great	1811		
Brightlingsea	1811	1831		Rainham	1801		
Clacton, Great	1811			Rochford	1811		
Colchester, St Leonard		1811	1821	Saffron Walden	1811		
Colne, Wakes	1809			Sandon	1811		
Debden	1801	1821		St Lawrence	1811		
Elmstead	1811			Steeple Bumpstead	1831		
Finchingfield	1821	1831		Terling	1801	1811	
Gestlingthorpe	1811			Thorrington	1811		
Harlow	1797			Tilbury juxta Clare	1811	1821	1831
Hatfield Broad Oak	1811			Tolleshunt Major	1821	1831	
Horndon on the Hill	1811	1821		Toppesfield	1811		

Upminster	1831		Witham	1811	
Walthamstow	1811	1821	Woodham Walter	1811	1831
Wanstead	1821		Wormingford	1831	
Wickford	1811		Writtle	1821	

ESSEX **1841**
Elmstead [ES/C2]
Panfield [ES/C 5]
Thaxted [ES/L 37]

The Society holds no microfilms for 1841

ESSEX **1851**
Essex FHS [Mfc] and East of London FHS 1851 Census Index [ELF]   * = Microfilm held

REGISTRATION DISTRICT	HO 107	Volume	Location
Billericay RD	1774*		Mfc
Braintree RD	1785*		Mfc
Chelmsford RD			
- Ingatestone & Chelmsford SDs	1775*		Mfc
- Writtle, Great Waltham & Great Baddow SDs	1776*		Mfc
Colchester RD	1781*		Mfc
Dunmow RD	*Returns missing*		
Epping RD	1770*		Mfc
Halstead RD	1784*		
Lexden RD	1782*		Mfc
Maldon RD	1778*		Mfc
Ongar RD	1771*		Mfc
Orsett RD	1773*		Mfc
Rochford RD	1777*		Mfc
Romford RD	1772*	ELF 1	ES/C 3
Saffron Walden RD	1786*		Mfc
Tendring & Harwich RD	1779-1780*		Mfc
West Ham RD	1768-1769*		
- Wanstead & Woodford parishes	1769*	ELF 8	ES/C 4
- Leyton & Walthamstow SDs	1769*		Mfc
Witham RD	1783*		

ESSEX **1851** 2% Sample [surname index] [Mfc]
Birchanger; Downham; Foulness; Havering atte Bower; Oakley, Little; Rivenhall

ESSEX **1861**
Hatfield Broad Oak [ES/C5]
Panfield [ES/C 5]

REGISTRATION DISTRICT	RG 9	* = Microfilm held
Linton RD - Essex part	1028-1030*	

ESSEX **1871**
Panfield [ES/C 5]
Walthamstow (Waltham Forest FHS J 1/5) [ES/PER]

ESSEX **1881**
GSU Transcript & Indexes - county complete [Lower Library Mfc]

GLOUCESTERSHIRE (GL)

1670, 1680, 1718, 1741 Westleigh manor survey [GL/L 63]
1696 Bristol (Bristol Rec Soc 25) [GL/PER]
1742 Olveston (J Bristol & Avon FHS 15) [GL/PER]
1767 GL papist return (CRS Occ Paper 2) [RC/PER]

GLOUCESTERSHIRE 1851 * = Microfilm held
Gloucestershire FHS [GLF]; Bristol & Avon FHS [BAF]; 1851 Census Indexes & GSU pilot project 1851 transcript & indexes of **Warwickshire** including cross county districts [GSW]

REGISTRATION DISTRICT	HO 107	Volume No	Location
Bristol RD			
- St Mary Redcliffe SD	1947*	BAF 4, 5	GL/C 1
- Castle Precincts SD	1948*	BAF 2, 3	GL/C 1
- St Paul SD	1949*		
- St James SD	1950*		
- St Augustine SD	1951*	BAF 6	GL/C 6
Cheltenham RD			
- Charlton Kings SD	1972*		
- Cheltenham SD	1973*	BAF 9	Mfc
Chipping Sodbury RD	1956*	BAF 17	Mfc
Cirencester RD	1968*	GLF 3	Mfc
Clifton RD			
- Clifton SD	1952*	BAF	GL/C 2-3
- Ashley SD	1953*		
- St George SD	1953*		
- SS Philip & Jacob SD	1954*	BAF 8a-c	GL/ C1
- Westbury SD	1955*		
- Stapleton SD	1955*		
Dursley RD	1958*		
Gloucester RD			
- Kingston & St Nicholas SDs	1961*	GLF 1	Mfc
- St John Baptist & South Hamlet SDs	1962*	GLF 2	Mfc
Newent RD	1960*		
Northleach RD	1969*	GLF 10	Mfc
Stow on the Wold RD	1970*		
Stroud RD			
- Stoneham, Painswick & Bisley SDs	1964*	GLF 5	Mfc
- Stroud & Rodborough SDs	1965*	GLF 6	Mfc
- Minchinhampton & Horsley SDs	1966*	GLF 7	Mfc
Tetbury RD	1967*	GLF 8	Mfc
Tewkesbury RD	1974*		
Thornbury RD	1957*	BAF 17	Mfc
Westbury on Severn RD	1959*		
Wheatenhurst RD	1963*	GLF 4	Mfc
Winchcombe RD	1971*		
Stratford on Avon RD - Gloucestershire part	2074	GSW	Mfc

GLOUCESTERSHIRE 1851 2% Sample (Surname index) [Mfc]
Clopton; Eastlach; Frocester; Itchington; Mickleton with Clopton; Preston; Stoke Gifford; Stowe on the Wold; Tirley; Turville;

GLOUCESTERSHIRE 1861
Bristol 1861 Census Index - Jane Baker [JB]   * = Microfilm held
REGISTRATION DISTRICT	RG 9		Location
Bristol RD			
- Castle Precincts SD	1715-1716*	JB	GL/C 5
- St James SD	1720-1721*	JB	GL/C 5
- St Mary Redcliffe SD	1712-1714*		
- St Paul SD	1717-1719*		
- St Augustine SD	1722-1724*		
Cheltenham RD			
- Charlton Kings SD	1794-1796*		
- Cheltenham SD	1797-1803*		
Chipping Sodbury RD	1743-1746*		
Cirencester RD	1781-1785*		
Clifton RD			
- Clifton SD	1725-1728*		
- Ashley SD	1729-1730*		
- St George SD	1731-1732*		
- SS Philip & Jacob SD	1733-1738*		
- Westbury SD	1739-1740*		
- Stapleton SD	1741-1742*		
Dursley RD	1750-1753*		
Gloucester RD	1763-1768*		
Newent RD	1759-1762*		
Northleach RD	1786-1788*		
Stow on the Wold RD	1789-1790*		
Stroud RD	1771-1780*		
Tetbury RD	1779-1780*		
Tewkesbury RD	1804-1807*		
Thornbury RD	1747-1749*		
Westbury on Severn RD	1754-1758*		
Wheatenhurst RD	1769-1770*		
Winchcombe RD	1791-1793*		

GLOUCESTERSHIRE 1871
Bristol 1871 Census Index - Jane Baker [JB]
REGISTRATION DISTRICT	RG 10		Location
Bristol RD			
- St Mary Redcliffe SD	2519-2521	JB	GL/C 1
- St Paul SD	2524-2529	JB	GL/C 1
- St Augustine SD	2532-2538	JB	GL/C 5
Clifton RD			
- St Philip & Jacob SD	2556-2566	JB	GL/C 5

GLOUCESTERSHIRE 1881
GSU Transcripts & Indexes - county complete [Mfc Lower Library]

GLOUCESTERSHIRE 1891
Oxfordshire FHS 1891 Census Index [OXF]
REGISTRATION DISTRICT	RG 12		Location
Farringdon RD - Gloucestershire part	0974-0976	OXF	Mfc

HAMPSHIRE (HA)

1582   Andover list (*males 12-70*) (Hist Andover Grammar Sch) [SCH/AND]
1767   HA papist return (CRS Occ Paper 2) [RC/PER]
1821   Ryde IoW [HA/C 12 & SP 25/1]

HAMPSHIRE 1841
Hamble [HA/R 30]
Hound [HA/R 38]

HAMPSHIRE 1851
Hampshire Genealogical Society 1851 Census Index Vol 1-68 [HAG]. Isle of Wight FHS 1851 Census Index [IOW]   * = Microfilm held
Hampshire Gen Soc 1851 census master name & place indexes [Mfc Shelf 9]

REGISTRATION DISTRICT	HO 107	Volume No	Location
Alresford RD	1678*	HAG 15, 22	HA/C 1-14
Alton RD	1679*	HAG 20, 24	HA/C 1-14
Alverstoke RD	1660*	HAG 35-37	HA/C 1-14
Andover RD	1683*	HAG 4,8,42	HA/C 1-14
Basingstoke RD	1681*	HAG 2,5-7,23	HA/C 1-14
Catherington RD	1677*	HAG 19, 25	HA/C 1-14
Christchurch RD	1667*	HAG 38	HA/C 1-14
Droxford RD	1676*	HAG 21, 26	HA/C 1-14
Fareham RD	1661*	HAG 31, 32	HA/C 1-14
Fordingbridge RD	1667*	HAG 19, 25	HA/C 1-14
Hartley Wintney RD	1680*	HAG 23. 34	HA/C 1-14
Havant RD	1656*	HAG 18	HA/C 1-14
Isle of Wight RD	1662-1665*	HAG 53-59	HA/C 1-14
Isle of Wight - Surname index to HAG 53-59		IOW	Mfc Shelf 9
Kingsclere RD	1684*	HAG 9, 10	HA/C 1-14
Lymington RD	1666*	HAG 61	HA/C 1-14
New Forest RD	1668*	HAG 27, 23, 60	HA/C 1-14
Petersfield RD	1677*	HAG 19, 25	HA/C 1-14
Portsea Island RD	1657-1659*	HAG 44-51	HA/C 1-14
Ringwood RD	1667*	HAG 28, 52	HA/C 1-14
Romsey RD	1671*	HAG 1, 13, 22	HA/C 1-14
Southampton RD	1669*	HAG 62-66	HA/C 1-14
South Stoneham RD	1670*	HAG 14, 16, 29	HA/C 1-14
Stockbridge RD	1672*	HAG 22, 30	HA/C 1-14
Whitchurch RD	1682*	HAG 17	HA/C 1-14
Winchester RD			
- Mitcheldever & Worthing SDs	1673*	HAG 3	HA/C 1-14
- Winchester SD	1674*	HAG 39-41	HA/C 1-14
- Twyford & Hursley SDs	1675*	HAG 11, 12	HA/C 1-14
Newbury RD - Hampshire part	1685*	HAG 67	HA/C 1-14
Hungerford RD - Hampshire part	1686*	HAG 67	HA/C 1-14
Farnborough RD - Hampshire part	1595-1596*	HAG 67, 68	HA/C 1-14
Bradfield RD - Hampshire part	1691*	HAG 23	HA/C 1-14

HAMPSHIRE 1851 2% Sample [surname index] [Mfc]
Beauworth; Chilbolton; Micheldever; Motistone; Rotherwick; Roughdown

HAMPSHIRE 1851 Religious Census
Hampshire Rec Ser Vol 12 [HA/PER]

HAMPSHIRE 1861   * = Microfilm held

REGISTRATION DISTRICT RG 9		REGISTRATION DISTRICT RG 9	
Alresford RD	0702-0703*	Kingsclere RD	0717-0718*
Alton RD	0704-1705*	Lymington RD	0663-0665
Alverstoke RD	0645-0648*	- Lymington SD	0663*
Andover RD	0713-0716*	New Forest RD	0670-0672
Basingstoke RD	0708-0711*	Petersfield RD	0700-0701*
Catherington RD	0699*	Portsea Island RD	0632-0644*
Christchurch RD	0666-0667	Ringwood RD	0668
Droxford RD	0696-0698*	Romsey RD	0685-0686*
Fareham RD	0649-0651*	Southampton RD	0673-0679*
Fordingbridge RD	0699	South Stoneham RD	0680-0684*
Hartley Wintney RD	0706-0707*	Stockbridge RD	0687-0688*
Havant RD	0631*	Whitchurch RD	0712*
Isle of Wight RD	0652-0662*	Winchester RD	0689-0695*

HAMPSHIRE 1881
GSU Transcripts & Indexes - county complete [Lower Library Mfc]

HAMPSHIRE 1891
Isle of Wight FHS [IOW] & Hampshire GS [HAG] 1891 Census Indexes

REGISTRATION DISTRICT	RG 12	Volume No	Location
Alverstoke RD	0878-0881	HAG 6	Mfc Shelf 9
Fareham RD	0882-0884	HAG 7	Mfc Shelf 9
Isle of Wight RD *part* -			
(Brightstone, Brook, Calbourne,			
Freshwater, Mottistone, Newtown,			
Shalfleet, Thorley & Yarmouth)	0897	IOW	HA/C 18
Portsea Island RD			
- Army	0853-0877		Mfc Shelf 9
- Havant SD	0851-0852	HAG 5	Mfc Shelf 9
- Kingston SD	0853-0860	HAG 3	Mfc Shelf 9
- Landport SD	0866-0877	HAG 4	Mfc Shelf 9
- Portsea Town	0861-0863	HAG 1	Mfc Shelf 9
- Portsmouth Town	0864-0865	HAG 2	Mfc Shelf 9
Ringwood & Fordingbridge RD	0908-0909	HAG 13	Mfc Shelf 9

HEREFORDSHIRE (HR)

1767 HR papist return (CRS Occ Paper 2) [RC/PER]

HEREFORDSHIRE 1841
The 1841 districts were based upon the Hundreds.
The Society has microfilms for the following Hundreds:
DISTRICT/HUNDRED   HO 107   DISTRICT/HUNDRED   HO 107
Broxash (*part*)/Ewyas-Lacey 419-420   Hereford City   433
Huntingdon/Radlow (*part*)   423-424

HEREFORDSHIRE 1841-1881
Huntington [Mfc]

HEREFORDSHIRE 1851
Herefordshire FHS 1851 Census Index [HEF]   * = Microfilm held

REGISTRATION DISTRICT	HO 107	Volume No	Location
Bromyard RD	1980		
Hereford RD	1977-1978	HEF	Mfc
Hereford RD	1978	HEF	Shelf 9
Ledbury RD	1975		
Leominster RD	1981	HEF	Mfc
Ross RD	1976	HEF	Mfc
Weobley RD	1979	HEF	Mfc
Ludlow RD - Herefordshire part	1982*	HEF	Mfc
Knighton RD - Herefordshire part	2493*		
Presteigne RD - Herefordshire part	2492*		
Tenbury RD - Herefordshire part	2040*	HEF	Mfc

HEREFORDSHIRE 1851 2% Sample (Surname index) [Mfc]
Cusop; How Caple; Kinsham Upper; Moccas; Richard's Castle; Withington

HEREFORDSHIRE 1861   * = Microfilm held

REGISTRATION DISTRICT	RG 9
Bromyard RD	1827-1829*
Hereford RD	1816-1824*
Ledbury RD	1808-1811*
Leominster RD	1830-1833*
Ross RD	1812-1815*
Weobley RD	1825-1826*

HEREFORDSHIRE 1881
GSU Transcripts & Indexes - county complete [Lower Library Mfc]

HERTFORDSHIRE (HT)

1767   HT papist return (CRS Occ Paper 2) [RC/PER]
1821   Thorley [HT/C 1]

HERTFORDSHIRE 1841
Croxley Green Extracts [HT/C 1]
Rickmansworth Extracts [HT/C 1]

HERTFORDSHIRE 1841
The 1841 districts were based upon the Hundreds.
The Society holds microfilms for the following Hundreds:

DISTRICT/HUNDRED	HO 107	DISTRICT/HUNDRED	HO 107
Braughlin	434	Dacorum/Edwinstree	441-443
Cashio	438	Odsey/Hertford & St Albans	446-447

HERTFORDSHIRE **1851**
Population, Economy & Family Structure in Hertfordshire. University of Hertfordshire 1851
Census Index [HTU]   * = Microfilm held
REGISTRATION DISTRICT   HO 107   Volume No   Location
Berkhampstead RD   1716*   HTU   HT/C 2
Bishops Stortford RD   1706*
Hatfield RD   1712*
Hemel Hempstead RD   1715*
Hertford RD   1711*
Hitchin RD   1709-1710*
Royston RD   1707-1708*
St Albans RD   1713*
Ware RD   1705*
Watford RD   1714*

HERTFORDSHIRE **1861**   * = Microfilm held
REGISTRATION DISTRICT   RG 9
Berkhampstead RD   0841-0843*
Bishops Stortford RD   0807-0810*
Hatfield RD   0825-0826*
Hemel Hempstead RD   0837-0840*
Hertford RD   0822-0824*
Hitchin RD   0816-0821*
Royston RD   0811-0815*
St Albans RD   0827-0831*
Ware RD   0803-0806*
Watford RD   0832-0836*

Luton RD - Hertfordshire part 1011*, 1015*

HERTFORDSHIRE **1861**
Barkway High Street [HT/C 1]
Sandridge [HT/C 1]

HERTFORDSHIRE **1871**
Barkway High Street [HT/C 1]

HERTFORDSHIRE **1881**
GSU Transcripts & Indexes - county complete [Lower Library Mfc]

HUNTINGDONSHIRE (HU)

1767   HU papist return (CRS Occ Paper 2) [RC/PER]

HUNTINGDONSHIRE **1841**
The districts were based upon the Hundreds.
The Society holds microfilms for the following Hundreds, county complete:
DISTRICT/HUNDRED   HO 107
Hurstingstone/Leightonstone   448-450
Leightonstone/Normancross   451-452
Toseland/Huntingdon   453-455

Censearch index to its own unpublished transcript - county complete [Mfc]

Cambridgeshire FHS Journal indexes [CFJ]
Huntingdon Union   (CFJ 3/7) [CA/PER]
St Ives Union   (CFJ 3/5) [CA/PER]
St Neots Union   (CFJ 3/6) [CA/PER]

HUNTINGDONSHIRE 1851
Cambridgeshire, Peterborough & Northamptonshire FHS 1851 Census Transcripts & Index
[CPN]; Cambridgeshire FHS Journal indexes [CFJ]   * = Microfilm held

REGISTRATION DISTRICT	HO 107	Volume No	Location
Huntingdon RD	1748*	CPN	HU/C 6, 7
Huntingdon RD	1748*	CFJ 3/7	CA/PER
St Ives RD	1749*	CPN	HU/C 2, 3
St Ives RD	1749*	CFJ 3/5	CA/PER
St Neots RD	1750*	CPN	HU/C 4, 5
St Neots RD	1750*	CFJ 3/6	CA/PER

Caxton RD - Huntingdonshire part   1758*
Peterborough RD
 - Huntingdonshire part   1747*   CPN   HU/C 1
Oundle RD - Huntingdonshire part   1746*   CPN   HU/C 6
Thrapston RD - Huntingdonshire part   1745*

HUNTINGDONSHIRE 1861
REGISTRATION DISTRICT   RG 9   * = Microfilm held
Huntingdon RD   0971-0975*
St Ives RD   0976-0980*
St Neots RD   0981-0984*

Caxton RD - Huntingdonshire part   1016-1017*

HUNTINGDONSHIRE 1881
Huntingdonshire FHS 1881 Census Index [HUF]

REGISTRATION DISTRICT	RG 11	Volume No	Location
Huntingdon RD	1600-1604	HUF 1.1	Mfc
St Ives RD	1605-1609	HUF 1.2	Mfc
St Neots RD	1610-1613	HUF 1.3	Mfc

HUNTINGDONSHIRE 1881
GSU Transcripts & Indexes - county complete [Lower Library Mfc]

KENT (KE)

1676 Wrotham & Stansted 'Compton' census (Archaeologia Cantiana 94)
      Stansted 'Compton' census (NW KE FH 2/7) [*both* KE/PER]
1767 KE papist return (CRS Occ Paper 2) [RC/PER]
1790 Hayes census (NW KE FH 4/4) [KE/PER]
c1800 Folkestone returns [KE/L 34]
1801 Bromley census (NW KE FH J 1/5) [KE/PER]
      Deal: St Leonard's census (KE FHS Rec Pub 177) [Mfc]
1811 Deal: St Leonard's census (KE FHS Rec Pub 177) [Mfc]

1821 Beckenham census (NW KE FH J 1/6) [KE/PER]
Deal: St Leonard's census (KE FHS Rec Pub 177) [Mfc]

KENT 1841-1881 [all years]
Kent FHS Record Series, 1841-1881 Census Indexes [KEF]; Index of Persons of Irish Birth by Peter Manning [KPM]

PARISH	Volume No	Location
Ashley, Northbourne	KEF 843	Mfc
Chatham	KPM	KE/C 2
Guston	KEF 836	Mfc
Kingsdown	KEF 846	Mfc
Langdon	KEF 840	Mfc
Oxney	KEF 839	Mfc
Poulton	KEF 834	Mfc
Ripple	KEF 844	Mfc
St Margaret at Cliffe	KEF 837	Mfc
Sholden	KEF 848	Mfc
Sutton by Dover	KEF 847	Mfc
Whitfield	KEF 835	Mfc

KENT 1841
Down [KE/C 1& 8]   Keston [KE/C 1]
Erith [KE/C 1]   Wickham, East [KE/C 1]
Farnborough [KE/C 1]   Wickham, West [KE/C 1& 7]

KENT 1851
North West Kent FHS 1851 Census Index [NWK]; Institute of Heraldic & Genealogical Studies 1851 Census Index [IHGS]; Kent FHS 1851 Census Indexes [KEF]; Martin Webster's Index of Dover [MW]   * = Microfilm held

REGISTRATION DISTRICT	HO 107	Volume No	Location
Blean RD	1625*		
Bridge RD	1623*		
Bromley RD	1606*	NWK 1	KE/C 8
Canterbury RD	1624		
Cranbrook RD	1619*		
Dartford RD	1607*	NWK 5	KE/C 9
Dover RD	1632*		
Dover RD [ff 110-810]	1632*	MW Pts 1-7	Mfc

- Dover Borough only - Gurston, Charlton nr Dover, Dover Castle, East Cliffe, Dover St James, Dover St Mary, Hougham, Buckland)

East Ashford RD	1622*		
Eastry RD	1631*		
Elham RD	1633		
Faversham RD	1626*		
Gravesend RD	1608		
Greenwich RD			
- Deptford SD	1584-1585*	NWK 3	KE/C 8
- Greeenwich SD	1886-1887*		Mfc
- Woolwich SD	1588-1589*	NWK 2	KE/C 8
Hollingbourne RD	1618*		
Hoo RD	1609		
Lewisham RD	1590-1591	NWK 4	KE/C 8
Maidstone RD	1616-1617		
Malling RD	1612		

Medway RD	1610-1611		
Milton RD	1627*		
North Aylesford RD	1609		
Romney Marsh RD	1634*		
Sevenoaks RD	1613*	NWK 6	KE/C 9
Sheppey RD	1628		
Tenterden RD	1620*		
Thanet RD	1629-1630	IHGS 1	Shelf 9
Tunbridge RD	1614-1615		
West Ashford RD	1621*		

KENT 1861
REGISTRATION DISTRICT   RG 9   * = Microfilm held
Greenwich RD
- Deptford St Paul SD (*part*)   0393-0396*
- Greenwich West SD   0398-0400*
- Greenwich East SD   0400-0403*
- Woolwich Dockyard SD   0404-0406*

KENT 1881
GSU Transcript & Indexes - county complete [Lower Library Mfc]

KENT 1891
J Breeze 1891 Census Index [KJB]
REGISTRATION DISTRICT	RG 12	Volume No	Location
Milton RD	0716-0719	KJB	KE/C 2

LANCASHIRE (LA)

- **1676** Broughton 'Compton' census (Recusant Hist 15/3) [RC/PER]
- **1705** LA papist return [RC/LST]
- **1767** LA papist return (CRS Occ Paper 1) [RC/PER]
- **1801** Bolton: Breightmet census (Manchester Gengst 23/3)
  Bury: Elton census (Manchester Gengst 20/4-21/1)
  Liverpool census extract (Trans Hist Soc La & CH 130)
  Turton: Edworth census (Manchester Gengst 11/2) [*all* LA/PER]
  Winwick with Hulme census (N CH FHn 5/1) [CH/PER]
- **1811** Great Bolton census (Mfc) [Apply to Staff]
- **1821** Great Bolton census (Mfc) [Apply to Staff]
- **1831** Great Bolton census (Mfc) [Apply to Staff]

LANCASHIRE 1841
The 1841 registration districts were based upon the Hundreds.
The Society holds microfilms for the following districts:

DISTRICT/HUNDRED	HO 107
Amoundemess *part*	495-496
Lonsdale	529-531
Salford - Rochdale *part*	552
Salford *part*	578-580, 581 bk 6-586
West Derby *part*	553 bk 3 - bk 9
Liverpool St Thomas *part*	565-566
Liverpool - Toxteth Park *part*	567-568
Manchester *part*	569-577

Parish indexes [LA/C 2]
Acton Grange; Aston by Sutton; Aston Grange; Bold; Clifton; Cronton; Cuerdley; Ditton; Hale; Halebank; Halton; Halton, South; Keckwick; Moore; Newton by Daresbury; Norton; Preston; Rainhill (part); Stockham; Sutton; Weston; Widnes

LANCASHIRE 1851
Manchester & Lancashire FHS/Lancashire FHHS joint publications [M/L];
Cumbria FHS [CUF]; Ormskirk FHS [OFH];
Warrington Group [WLV] & Liverpool & District FHS [LIV] 1851 Census Indexes

Index to townships in M/L surname index of Lancashire [LA/C 8]
Cumbrians in Liverpool (HO 107/2176-2185) (CUF) [LA/C 17]
Cumbrians in West Derby (2186-2192) (CUF) [LA/C 17]

* = Microfilm held

REGISTRATION DISTRICT	HO 107	Volume No	Location
Ashton under Lyne RD	**2233-2339**		
- Ashton under Lyne SD	2233	M/L 18	LA/C 5
- Droylsden/Audenshaw/Denton SDs	2234-2235	M/L 13	LA/C 4
- Newton & Dukinfield SDs	2236-2237	M/L 19	LA/C 5
- Hartshead/Mottram& Staly SDs	2238-2239	M/L 20	LA/C 5
Barton on Irwell RD	**2217-2218**		
- Barton/Stretford & Worsley SDs	2217-2218	M/L 12	LA/C 4
Blackburn RD	**2257-2261**		
- Billington/Harwood/Mellor SDs	2257		
- Blackburn SD (*part*)	2258	M/L 37	LA/C 6
- Blackburn SD (*part*)	2259	M/L 38	Mfc
- Oswaldtwistle SD	2260	M/L 39	LA/C 6
- Darwen/Witton SDs	2261		
Bolton RD	**2206-2211**		
- Farnworth/Hulton SDs	2206*	M/L 56	LA/C 8
- Westhoughton/Halliwell/Horwich SDs	2207	M/L 56	LA/C 8
- Tongwith/Haulgh/Turton/Edgeworth & Sharpley SDs	2208*	M/L 56	LA/C 8
- Bolton Gt & Lt/Lever/Darcy Lever SDs	2209-2211*	M/L 55	LA/C 8
Burnley RD	**2251-2254**		
- Burnley/Padiham SDs	2251-2253		
- Colne/Pendle SDs	2254	M/L 35	LA/C 6
Bury RD	**2212-2216**		
- Holcombe/Tottington Lower End SDs	2212*	M/L 25	LA/C 5
- Birtle/Heywood SDs	2213*		
- South Bury SD	2214	M/L 27	LA/C 5
- North Bury/Elton SDs	2215	M/L 28	LA/C 5
- Radcliff/Pilkington SDs	2216	M/L 29	Mfc
Chorley RD	**2262-2263**		
- Brindle/Leyland/Rivington SDs	2262	M/L 54	LA/C 8
- Chorley]/Croston SDs	2263	M/L 51	LA/C 6
Chorlton RD	**2219-2221**		
- Didsbury SD	2219	M/L 9	LA/C 3
- Chorlton SD	2220	M/L 10	LA/C 4
- Chorlton upon Medlock (unfilmed *part*)	2220	M/L 10 sup	Mfc
- Hulme SD	2221	M/L 8	LA/C 3
- Hulme SD (unfilmed *part*)	2221	M/L 8 sup	Mfc
Clitheroe RD	**2255-2256**		
- Slaidburn/Chipping/Clitheroe & Whalley SDs	2255-2256	M/L 41-2	LA/C 6

Fylde RD 2269
  - Kirkham/Lytham/Poulton le Fylde SDs   2269   M/L 43   LA/C 6
Garstang RD   2270
  - Stalmine/St Michael/Garstang SDs   2270   M/L 44   LA/C 6
Haslingdon RD   2248-2250
  - Newchurch SD   2248   M/L 30   LA/C 5
  - Rossendale & Edenfield SDs   2249
  - Haslingdon & Accrington SDs   2250   M/L 32   LA/C 5
Lancaster RD   2271-2273
  - Ellel/Heaton SDs   2271   M/L 45   LA/C 6
  - Slyne & Hest, Halton with Aughton Bulk,
    Skerton, Lancaster Castle, Aldercliffe
    Ashton with Stoday & Scotforth   2272   M/L 46   LA/C 6
  - Caton/Wray/Tunstall/ Arkholme &
    Warton SDs   2273   M/L 57   LA./C 8
Leigh RD   2204-2205
  - Lowton/Culcheth/West Leigh &
    Atherton SDs   2204-2205   M/L 17   LA/C 5
Liverpool RD   2176-2185   LIV 1-34   LA/C 11-15
Liverpool - Guide to EDs   LIV   LA/C 11
Manchester RD   2225-2232
  - Ancoates SD   2225-2226   M/L 5   LA/C 3
  - Deansgate SD   2227*   M/L 6   LA/C 3
  - Deansgate SD (unfilmed *part*)   2227   M/L 60   Mfc
  - London Road SD   2228   M/L 3,53   LA/C 3,6
  - London Road SD (unfilmed *part*)   2228   M/L 3 sup   Mfc
  - Market Street SD   2229   M/L 2   LA/C 3
  - St Georges SD   2230   M/L 4   LA/C 3
  - Newton/Beswick/Bradford SDs   2231   M/L 1   LA/C 3
  - Cheetham/Failsworth SDs   2232   M/L 7   LA/C 3
Oldham RD   2240-2243
  - Oldham SD   2240-2241   M/L 47   LA/C 6
  - Middleton/Chadderton/Royton
    & Crompton SDs   2242-2243   M/L 48   LA/C 6
Ormskirk RD   2196-2197
  - Bickerstaffe/Aughton/Hallsall/
    Fornby/North Meols SDs   2196*   OFH   LA/C 1
  - Tarleton/Scarisbrick/Ormskirk/
    Lathom SDs   2197*   OFH   LA/C 1
Prescot RD   2193-2195
  - Hale/MuchWootton/Huyton/Farnworth/
    Prescot/St Helens/Rainford SDs   2193-2195
Preston RD   2264-2268
  - Longton SD   2264   M/L 50   LA/C 6
  - Preston SD   2265-2267   M/L 49   LA/C 6
  - Walton le Dale/Alston/Broughton SDs   2268   M/L 58   LA/ C8
Rochdale RD   2244-2247
  - Butterworth/Castleton SDs   2244   M/L 21   LA/C 5
  - Spotland SD   2245   M/L 22   LA/C 5
  - Wardleworth/Wuerdle SDs   2246   M/L 23   LA/C 5
  - Whitworth/Blatchinworth SDs   2247
Salford RD   2222-2224
  - Pendleton/Broughton/Greengates/
    Regent Road SDs   2222-2224   M/L 11   LA/C 4
  - Greengates SD (unfilmed *part*)   2223   M/L 11sup   Mfc

Ulverston RD	2274-2275		
- Cartmel/Colton/Ulverston SDs	2274	LFHHS	Mfc
- Ulverston [ff 5-96]	2274	CUF	LA/C 18
- Ulverston [ff 126-245]	2275	CUF	LA/C 18
- Dalton/West Broughton & Hawkshead SDs	2275		
Warrington RD	2202-2203		
- Newton in Mackerfield/ Winwick/Sankey/ Warrington/Latchford/ Rixton SDs	2202-2203*	WLV	Shelf 9
West Derby RD	2186-2192		
West Derby - Guide to EDs			Shelf 9
+ = indexes in progress - ask staff for all published so far			
- Toxteth Park SD	2186-2188	LIV35-45	Mfc+
- Everton SD	2189-2190	LIV46-50	Mfc+
- Walton/Crosby/Litherland SDs	2191	LIV51-52	Mfc+
- West Derby/Wavertree SDs	2192	LIV52-59	Mfc+
Wigan RD	2198-2201		
- Standish/Aspull/Wigan/Hindley/Pemberton/ Upholland/Ashton in Mackerfield SDs	2198-2201	M/L 14-16	LA/C 4

LANCASHIRE 1851 2% Sample [surname index] [Mfc]
Bucklebury; Cumnor; Emborne; Fernham; Isley West

LANCASHIRE 1861
Lancashire FHHS 1861 Census Surname Indexes [Mfc]
Please ask staff for Piece Number index. All districts listed.   * = Microfilm held

REGISTRATION DISTRICT	RG 9	Location
Ashton under Lyne RD	2977-3066	
Barton in Irwell RD	2859-2866*	
Blackburn RD	3089-3113	
- Billington, Harwood, Mellor, Oswaldtwistle,Darwen SDs	3089-3109*	
Bolton RD		
- Farnworth, Hulton, Westhoughton SDs	2807-2811	
- Little Bolton, Bolton Eastern, Bolton Western, Lever SDs	2820-2836*	
Burnley RD	3065-3082	
Bury RD	2837-2858*	
Chorley RD	3114-3123	
Chorlton RD	2867-2901*	
Clitheroe RD	3083-3088*	
- Clitheroe SD	3085*	Mfc
Fylde RD	3145-3150	
- Kirkham SD/Lytham Sds	3145-3147*	Mfc
- Poulton le Fylde SD	3148-3150*	Mfc
Garstang RD	3151*-3153*	
- Stalmine SD	3151*	Mfc
- St Michaels SD	3152*	Mfc
- Garstang SD	3153*	Mfc
Haslingden RD	3052-3064*	
- Rossendale & Spotland SDs	3057*	Mfc
Lancaster RD	3154-3164	
- Lancaster SD	3154-3163	Mfc
- Warton SD	3164	Mfc

Leigh RD	2799-2806	
- Lowton SD	2799*	
Liverpool RD	2650-2696*	
Manchester RD	2927-2976*	
Oldham RD	3007-3031	
Ormskirk RD	2756-2766	
- Bickerstaffe, Aughton, Halsall, Formby,		
North Meols, Tarleton, Scarisbrick SDs	2756-2764*	
Prescot RD	2739-2755	
- Farnworth, Precot, St Helens,		
Rainford SDs	2742-2755*	
Preston RD	3124-3144	
- Preston SD	3126-3144	Mfc
- Preston SD *part*	3126-3137*	
Rochdale RD	3032-3051	
Salford RD	2902-2926	
- Pendleton *part*, Broughton, Greengate,		
Regent Road SDs	2907-2926*	
- Regent Road *part* SD	2921-2924	LA/C 7
Ulverston RD	3165-3173	Mfc
Warrington RD	2787-2798*	
West Derby RD	2697-2738	
- Toxteth Park,Everton Walton &		
Crosby SDs	2697-2725*	
- West Derby *part*, Wavertree SDs	2728-2737*	
Wigan RD	2767-2786	

LANCASHIRE **1871**
Lancashire FHHS 1871 Census Surname Indexes [Mfc]
Please ask staff for Piece Number index . Only indexed RDs listed.   No microfilms held.

REGISTRATION DISTRICT	RG 10	Location
Clitheroe RD	4160-4167	Mfc
Fylde RD		
- Kirkham SD	4219-4220	Mfc
- Lytham SD	4221	Mfc
- Poulton le Fylde SD	4222-4224	Mfc
Garstang RD		
- Stalmine SD	4225	Mfc
- St Michaels SD	4226	Mfc
- Garstang SD	4227	Mfc
Haslingdon RD		
- Rawtenstall SD	4130-4134,4138	Mfc
Lancaster RD		
- Ellil SD	4228	Mfc
- Heaton SD	4229	Mfc
- Lancaster	4230-4232	Mfc
- Warton SD	4233	Mfc
Lunesdale RD		
- Caton Sd	4234	Mfc
- Wray SD	4235	Mfc
- Tunstal	4236	Mfc
- Arkholme	4237	Mfc
- Cartmel	4238	Mfc
- Colton SD	4239	Mfc

Preston RD
- Preston SD   4202-4213   Mfc
- Walton le Dale SD   4214-4215   Mfc
- Alston SD   4216   Mfc
- Broughton SD   4217-4218   Mfc

Ulverston RD
- Ulverston SD   4240-4241   Mfc
- Dalton SD   4242-4245   Mfc
- Broughton   4246   Mfc
- Hawkshead   4247   Mfc

LANCASHIRE 1881
GSU Transcripts & Indexes - county complete [Lower Library Mfc]

LANCASHIRE 1891
Lancashire FHHS 1891 Census Surname Indexes [Mfc].
Please ask staff for Piece Number index. Only indexed RDs listed.   No microfilms held.

REGISTRATION DISTRICT	RG 12	Location
Barrow in Furness RD		
- Barrow in Furness SD *part*	3482 & 3484	Mfc
- Barrow in Furness SD *part*	3486-3487	Mfc
Chorley RD		
- Brindle/Houghton/Wheelton/Withnell SDs	3419	Mfc
- Leyland SD	3420	Mfc
- Leyland/Euxton/Whittle le Woods/Cuerdon/ Clayton le Woods SDs	3421	Mfc
- Rivington/Adlington/ Heath Charnock & Anderton SDs	3422	Mfc
- Chorley SD	3423-3425	Mfc
- Chorley/Heapey/Duxbury/Coppull/Welch Whittle/Charnock Richard SDs	3426	Mfc
Fylde RD		
- Kirkham SD	3449-3451	Mfc
- Blackpool SD	3452-3455	Mfc
- Fleetwood	3456-3458	Mfc
Garstang RD		
- Stalmine SD	3459	Mfc
- St Michaels SD	3460	Mfc
- Garstang SD	3461	Mfc
Lancaster RD		
- Ellell SD	3462	Mfc
- Heaton SD	3463	Mfc
- Lancaster	3464-3468	Mfc
- Warton SD	3469	Mfc
Lunesdale RD		
- Caton SD	3470	Mfc
- Wray SD	3471	Mfc
- Tunstal SD	3472	Mfc
- Arkholme SD	3473	Mfc
- Cartmel SD	3474	Mfc
- Colton SD	3475	Mfc
Preston RD		
- Longton SD	3428	Mfc
- Trinity SD	3429-3433	Mfc

- St Peter SD	3434-3439	Mfc
- St John SD	3440-3443	Mfc
- Walton le Dale SD	3444-3445	Mfc
- Alston SD	3446	Mfc
- Broughton SD	3447-3448	Mfc
Ulverston RD		
- Ulverston SD	3476-3479	Mfc
- West Broughton SD	3480	Mfc
- Hawkshead SD	3481	Mfc
Wigan RD		
- Standish SD	3045-3046	Mfc
- Aspull/Blackrod/Heigh & Shipping SDs	3047-3048	Mfc
- Wigan SD	3049-3056	Mfc
- Hindley SD *part*	3057-3059	Mfc
- Hindley/Ince in Makefield SDs	3060-3062	Mfc

Coppul [LA/C 16]

LEICESTERSHIRE (LE)

LEICESTERSHIRE 1841
The 1841 districts were based upon the Hundreds.
The Society holds microfilms for the following Hundreds:

DISTRICT/HUNDRED	HO 107	DISTRICT/HUNDRED	HO 107
Framland/Gartree	588-591	Guthlaxton	598
Goscote, East	592-593	Sparkenhoe	600-603
Goscote, West	594-596	Leicester Borough	604-645

LEICESTERSHIRE 1851
Leicestershire FHS 1851 Census Index [LEF]; Lincolnshire FHS 1851 Census Index [LIF] & GSU pilot project 1851 transcript & indexes of **Warwickshire** including cross county districts [GSW].   * = Microfilm held

REGISTRATION DISTRICT	HO 107	Volume No	Location
Ashby de la Zouch RD	2084*	LEF 7-9,12	LE/C3
Barrow upon Soar RD	2087*	LEF 13,14, 21, 23	LE/C4-5
Billesdon RD	2080*	LEF 11	LE/C3
Blaby RD	2081*	LEF 10,4	LE/C3 & 2
Hinckley RD	2082*	LEF 5,6	LE/C2
Leicester RD	2088-2090*		
Loughborough RD	2085-2086*	LEF 15-17,8	LE/C4 & 3
Lutterworth RD	2078*	LEF 18,19	LE/C4
Market Bosworth RD	2083*	LEF 1,2	LE/C2
Market Harborough RD	2079*	LEF 3	LE/C2
Melton Mowbray RD	2091*	LEF 22,24-26	LE/C5
Atherstone RD - Leicestershire part	2064*	LEF 8 & GSW	LE/C3,Mfc
Bingham RD - Leicestershire part	2139*	LEF 22	LE/C5
Gt Easton RD - Leicestershire part	2093*	LEF 27	LE/C5
Grantham RD - Leicestershire part	2102-2103*	LIF 9	LI/C3
Oakham RD - Leicestershire part	2092*	LEF 27	LE/C5
Shardlow RD - Leicestershire part	2140	LEF 20	LE/C5

LEICESTERSHIRE 1851 2% Sample [Surname Index] [Mfc]
Barkby; Barton in the Beans; Bescaby; Glenfield; Keythorpe; Knaptoft; Knipton; Upton

LEICESTERSHIRE 1861   * = Microfilm held
REGISTRATION DISTRICT RG 9   REGISTRATION DISTRICT RG 9
Ashby de la Zouch RD   2267-2272* Loughborough RD   2273-2278*
Barrow upon Soar RD   2279-2282* Lutterworth RD   2244-2248*
Billesdon RD   2253-2254* Market Bosworth RD   2263-2266*
Blaby RD   2255-2258* Market Harborough RD   2263-2266*
Hinckley RD   2259-2262* Melton Mowbray RD   2299-2304*
Leicester RD   2283-2298*

Barkeston [NT/C 5]
Birstall [LE/C 1]
Plungar [NT/C 5]

LEICESTERSHIRE 1871
Barkeston [NT/C 7B]
Barrow upon Soar [LE/C 1]
Bottesford [LI/C 4]
Knipton [LI/C 4]
Plungar [NT/C 7B]

LEICESTERSHIRE 1881
GSU Transcript & Indexes - county complete [Lower Library Mfc]

LEICESTERSHIRE 1891
Croxton-Keyrial [LI/C 8]
Hartson [LI/C 8]
Knipton [LI/C 8]
Muston [LI/C 8]
Redmile [LI/C 8]

LINCOLNSHIRE (LI)

1767 LI papist return (CRS Occ Paper 2) [RC/PER]
1771 Swinderby census (LI FHS Mag 4/1) [LI/PER]
1791 Swinderby census (LI FHS Mag 4/2) [LI/PER]
1831 Grantham: St Wulfram census (Mfc) [Apply to Staff]
1838 Marsh Chapel 1838 (LI FHS Mag 3/3-4) [LI/PER]

LINCOLNSHIRE 1841
Lincolnshire FHS 1841 Census Index [LIF] HO/107 606-651
The original returns were based upon the Lincolnshire Parts and Wapentakes.
Lincolnshire FHS has arranged the indexes into the following districts (based upon the later
Registration Districts)

DISTRICT	Location	DISTRICT	Location
Boston	Mfc	Horncastle	Mfc
Bourne	Mfc	Lincoln	Mfc
Caistor	Mfc	Louth	Mfc
Gainsborough	Mfc	Sleaford	Mfc
Glanford Brigg	Mfc	Spalding	Mfc
Grantham	Mfc	Spilsby	Mfc
Holbeach	Mfc	Stamford	Mfc

The Society holds microfilms for the following Parts &/or Wapentakes:
DISTRICT/WAPENTAKE   HO 107
Elloe, Kirton & Skirbeck   606-612
Boston   613
Parts of Kesteven   614-624
Grantham & Stanford Boroughs   625
Parts of Lindsey   626-636

LINCOLNSHIRE 1851
Lincolnshire FHS 1851 Census Index [LIF]   * = Microfilm held

REGISTRATION DISTRICT	HO 107	Volume No	Location
Boston RD	2098-2099*	LIF 12	LI/C 3
Bourne RD	2095*	LIF 10	LI/C 3
Caistor RD	2113-2115*	LIF 3	LI/C 2
Gainsborough RD	2119-2120*	LIF 1	LI/C 2
Glanford Brigg RD	2116-2118*	LIF 2	LI/C 2
Grantham RD	2102-2103*	LIF 5	LI/C 2
Holbeach RD	2097	LIF 11	LI/C 3
Horncastle RD	2107-2108*	LIF 4	LI/C 2
Lincoln RD	2104-2106*	LIF 6	LI/C 2
Louth RD	2111-2112*	LIF 5	LI/C 2
Sleaford RD	2100-2101*	LIF 8	LI/C 3
Spalding RD	2096	LIF 11	LI/C 3
Spilsby RD	2109-2110*	LIF 7	LI/C 3
Stamford RD	2094	LIF 10	LI/C 3
Goole RD - Lincolnshire part	2350*	LIF 1	LI/C 2
Newark RD - Lincolnshire part	2136*,2138*	LIF 1	LI/C 2
Peterborough RD - Lincolnshire part	1714*	LIF 1	LI/C 2
Thorne RD - Lincolnshire part	2349*	LIF 1	LI/C 2

LINCOLNSHIRE 1861
Lincolnshire FHS 1861 Census Index [LIF]   * = Microfilm held

REGISTRATION DISTRICT	RG 9	Volume No	Location
Boston RD	2331-2340*	LIF 10	Mfc
Bourne RD	2315-2319*	LIF 8	Mfc
Caistor RD	2388-2396*	LIF 1	Mfc
Gainsborough RD	2405-2411	LIF 12	Mfc
- Owston SD	2405*		
Glanford Brigg RD	2397-2404	LIF 7	Mfc
- Winterton & Barford SDs	2400-2404*		
Grantham RD	2347-2353*	LIF 5	Mfc
Holbeach RD	2326-2330*	LIF 11	Mfc
Horncastle RD	2365-2371	LIF 2	Mfc
Lincoln RD	2354-2364*	LIF 9	Mfc
Louth RD	2397-2387*	LIF 13	Mfc
Sleaford RD	2341-2346*	LIF 14	Mfc
Spalding RD	2320-2325*	LIF 3	Mfc
Spilsby RD	2372-2386*	LIF 6	Mfc
Stamford RD	2311-2314*	LIF 4	Mfc
Goole RD - Lincolnshire part	3526*	LIF 12	Mfc
Newark RD - Lincolnshire part	2481-2482*	LIF 12	Mfc
Peterborough RD - Lincolnshire part	968*	LIF 3	Mfc

Thorne RD - Lincolnshire part   3523*, 3526*   LIF 12   Mfc

LINCOLNSHIRE **1871**
Lincolnshire FHS 1871 Census Index [LIF]

REGISTRATION DISTRICT	RG 10	Volume No	Location
Boston RD	3333-3346	LIF 5	LI/C 4
Bourne RD	3311-3317	LIF 2	LI/C 4
Caistor RD	3411-3426	LIF 12	LI/C 5
Gainsborough RD	3439-3449	LIF 14	LI/C 5
Glanford Brigg RD	3427-3438	LIF 13	LI/C 5
Grantham RD	3354-3364	LIF 7	LI/C 4
Holbeach RD	3326-3332	LIF 4	LI/C 4
Horncastle RD	3378-3386	LIF 9	LI/C 5
Lincoln RD	3364-3377	LIF 8	LI/C 5
Louth RD	3398-3410	LIF 11	LI/C 5
Sleaford RD	3347-3353	LIF 6	LI/C 4
Spalding RD	3318-3325	LIF 3	LI/C 4
Spilsby RD	3387-3397	LIF 10	LI/C 5
Stamford RD	3307-3310	LIF 1	LI/C 4
Isle of Axholme RD	4725, 4728-9	LIF 14	LI/C 5
Newark RD - Lincolnshire part	3359,3540, 3544-45	LIF 6	LI/C 4
Peterborough RD - Lincolnshire part	1520	LIF 3	LI/C 4

LINCOLNSHIRE **1881**
Lincolnshire FHS 1881 Census Index [LIF]

REGISTRATION DISTRICT	RG 11	Volume No	Location
Boston RD	3212-3220	LIF 5	LI/C 6
Bourne RD	3195-3199	LIF 2	LI/C 6
Caistor RD	3267-3282	LIF 12	LI/C 7
Gainsborough RD	3292-3298	LIF 14	LI/C 7
Glanford Brigg RD	3283-3291	LIF 13	LI/C 7
Grantham RD	3227-3234	LIF 7	LI/C 6
Holbeach RD	3207-3211	LIF 4	LI/C 6
Horncastle RD	3247-3252	LIF 9	LI/C 7
Lincoln RD	3235-3246	LIF 8	LI/C 7
Louth RD	3260-3266	LIF 11	LI/C 7
Sleaford RD	3221-3226	LIF 6	LI/C 6
Spalding RD	3200-3206	LIF 3	LI/C 6
Spilsby RD	3253-3259	LIF 10	LI/C 7
Stamford RD	3191-3194	LIF 1	LI/C 6
Isle of Axholme RD - Lincolnshire part	4696,4699-4700	LIF 14	LI/C 7
Newark RD - Lincolnshire part	3373-3374, 3378-3379	LIF 6	LI/C 6
Peterborough RD - Lincolnshire part	1597	LIF 3	LI/C 6

LINCOLNSHIRE **1881**
GSU Transcripts & Indexes - county complete [Lower Library]

LINCOLNSHIRE **1891**
Lincolnshire FHS 1891 Census Index [LIF]

REGISTRATION DISTRICT	RG 12	Volume No	Location
Boston RD	2570-2576	LIF 5	LI/C 8
Bourne RD	2555-2558	LIF 2	LI/C 8

Caistor RD	2612-2624	LIF 12	LI/C 9
Gainsborough RD	2631-2637	LIF 14	LI/C 9
Glanford Brigg RD	2625-2630	LIF 13	LI/C 9
Grantham RD	2582-2586	LIF 7	LI/C 8
Holbeach RD	2566-2569	LIF 4	LI/C 8
Horncastle RD	2597-2600	LIF 9	LI/C 9
Lincoln RD	2587-2596	LIF 8	LI/C 8
Louth RD	2606-2611	LIF 11	LI/C 9
Sleaford RD	2577-2581	LIF 6	LI/C 8
Spalding RD	2559-2565	LIF 3	LI/C 8
Spilsby RD	2601-2605	LIF 10	LI/C 9
Stamford RD	2552-2554	LIF 1	LI/C 8
Isle of Axholme RD	3868,3870,3871	LIF 14	LI/C 9
Newark RD - Lincolnshire part	2711,2712, 2725,2726	LIF 6	LI/C 8
Peterborough RD - Lincolnshire part	1232	LIF 3	LI/C 8

LONDON and MIDDLESEX (MX)

1599 Ealing census (Ealing Loc Hist Soc Members Papers 2) [MX/C 20]
1695 London census (London Rec Soc 2) [MX/PER]
1733-34 London: St Mary Aldermanbury census (Harleian Soc Registers 5) [MX/R 5]
1767 MX papist return (CRS Occ Paper 2) [RC/PER]
1801 Chiswick 1801 [MX/C 5]
Ealing & Old Brentford census [MX/C 19];
Westminster: St James's Piccadilly census ext. (Great Marlborough Ward) [MX/C 2]
1810 New Brentford census (W MX FHS J 2/2 or 11/1) [MX/PER]
1811 Ealing & Old Brentford census [MX/C 19]
Hackney census (Parish Rets Sers 1) [MX/C 20]
1831 Poplar census (Parish Rets Sers 3) [MX/L 100 & MX/C 20]
Hackney census (Parish Rets Ser 2) [MX/C 20]

English Census Street Indexes - LONDON (Descent 16/2) [AUA/PER]

LONDON/MIDDLESEX **1841**
Metropolitan Area Street Index HO 107/659-741[mfc]
Censearch index to its own unpublished transcript Vols 1 & 2 [mfc]

The 1841 districts were based upon the Hundreds.
The Society has microfilms for the following Hundreds:
DISTRICT/HUNDRED   **HO 107**
Oulston - Finsbury St Luke   665
Oulston - Finsbury St Mary Islington West   667

LONDON/MIDDLESEX **1851**
London & North Middlesex FHS [LNM]; Central Middlesex FHS [CMX]; West Middlesex FHS [WMX]; East of London FHS [ELF]; Cliff Webb [CW] 1851 Census Indexes.
See also map showing Greater London RDs from staff at library enquiry counter
CENTRAL DISTRICTS OF LONDON 1851   * = Microfilm held

REGISTRATION DISTRICT	HO 107	Volume	Location
Clerkenwell RD	1516-1519	LNM	Mfc
East London RD	1524-1525	LNM 7	Mfc
Holborn RD	1513-1515	LNM 10	Mfc

REGISTRATION DISTRICT	HO 107	Volume	Location
London City RD	1528-1532	LNM 1	Mfc
London City RD	1530		MX/C 1
St Giles RD	1507-1509	LNM 9	Mfc
St Luke's RD	1520-1523	LNM 6	Mfc
Strand RD			
- St Anne Soho, Westminster SD	1510	LNM	Mfc
- St Mary le Strand SD	1511	LNM	Mfc
- St Clement Danes SD	1512	LNM	Mfc
West London RD	1526-1727	LNM	Mfc

EAST DISTRICTS OF LONDON 1851

REGISTRATION DISTRICT	HO 107	Volume	Location
Bethnal Green RD	1539-1542	ELF 2-5	Mfc & MX/C 3-4
Poplar RD	1555-1556		
Shoreditch RD	1533-1538	ELF 7	Mfc & MX/C 11
Stepney RD	1550-1554	CW	Mfc & MX/C7
St George in the East RD	1547-1549	ELF 6	Mfc & MX/C 11
Whitechapel RD	1543-1546		

NORTH DISTRICTS OF LONDON 1851

REGISTRATION DISTRICT	HO 107	Volume	Location
Hackney RD	1503-1506		
Hampstead RD	1492	LNM 2	Mfc
Islington RD	1499-1502	LNM	Mfc
Marylebone RD	1486-1491	LNM 3	Mfc
Pancras RD	1493-1498	LNM 2	Mfc

WEST DISTRICTS OF LONDON 1851

REGISTRATION DISTRICT	HO 107	Volume	Location
Chelsea RD	1472-1474	WMX 3	Mfc Shelf 9
Kensington RD			
- Paddington SD	1466-1467	WMX 1	Mfc Shelf 9
- Brompton, Hammersmith & Fulham SDs	1468-1471	WMX 2	Mfc Shelf 9
- Brompton SD	1468*		
St George Hanover Sq RD			
- Hanover Sq SD	1475	LNM	Mfc
- Mayfair SD	1476	LNM	Mfc
- Belgrave SD	1477-1478	LNM	Mfc
St James Westminster RD			
- Berwick Street SD	1483	LNM	Mfc
- St James Square SD	1484	LNM	Mfc
- Golden Square SD	1485	LNM	Mfc
St Martins in the Field RD			
- Charing Cross SD	1481	LNM	Mfc
- Long Acre SD	1482	LNM	Mfc
Westminster RD			
- St John SD	1479	LNM	Mfc
- St Margaret SD	1480	LNM	Mfc

MIDDLESEX EXTRA METROPOLITAN 1851
REGISTRATION DISTRICT			HO 107			Volume		Location
Barnet RD
 - Friern Barnet, Finchley, Monkton
   Hadley, South Mimms			1701			LNM 5		Mfc
Brentford RD
 - Isleworth/Twickenham SDs		1698			WMX 4		Mfc Shelf 9
 - Acton/Brentford/Chiswick SDs		1699			WMX		MX/C 20
Edmonton RD
 - Hornsey & Tottenham			1702			LNM 5		Mfc
 - Enfield & Edmonton			1703			LNM 5		Mfc
 - Waltham Abbey & Cheshunt SDs
   (Middlesex part)				1704			LNM 5		Mfc
Hendon RD
 - Kingsbury, Hendon, Willesden, Harrow,
   Great Stanmore, Little Stanmore,
   Edgware, Twyford, Pinner		1700			LNM 5		Mfc
Kingston RD
 - Hampton & Teddington SDs
   (Middlesex part)				1604*			WMX 4		Mfc Shelf 9
Staines RD
 - Staines & Sunbury SDs			1696			WMX		MX/C 20
Uxbridge RD
 - Ruislip, Hayes, Harefield, Hillingdon,
   West Drayton,Cowley, Ickenham,
   Norwood, Northholt			1697			WMX 5		Mfc

LONDON/MIDDLESEX **1861**
TC Barns 1861 Census Indexes
REGISTRATION DISTRICT			RG 9				Location
St Pancras RD
 - Somers Town SD				109-114				Mfc & MX/C 21
 - Camden Town SD				109,115-124			Mfc & MX/C 18
 - Kentish Town SD				119-124				Mfc & MX/C 13-16
 - Tottenham Court SD			100-103				Mfc & MX/C 22
 - Grays Inn SD					104-108				Mfc & MX/C 23
 - Regents Park SD				094-099				in progress

Parish indexes
Feltham [MX/C 8]
Kentish Town [MX/C 16]

LONDON/MIDDLESEX **1861**
Westminster & Central Middlesex FHS 1861 census indexes [CMX]		* = Microfilm held
REGISTRATION DISTRICT			RG 9					Location
Barnet RD *part*				797-789*
Brentford RD				771-781*
Edmonton RD *part*			794-802*
Hendon RD					782-786*
 - Willesden SD					785*			CMX		Mfc
Islington RD
 - Islington West SD				127-129*
Shoreditch RD *part*			231-243*

LONDON/MIDDLESEX **1871**
Clive Ayton 1871 Census Index
REGISTRATION DISTRICT   RG 10   Location
Kensingston RD
 - St John Paddington SD   019   MX/C 9
Westminster RD
 - Golden Square SD   136-139   MX/C 9
Pancras RD
 - Regents Park SD   199-203   MX/C 9
 - Grays Inn Lane SD   213   MX/C 9
Islington RD
 - Islington East SD   296   MX/C 9
Shoreditch RD
 - Haggerstone West SD   461-468   MX/C 9
Bethnal Green RD
 - Green SD   481-485   MX/C 9

LONDON/MIDDLESEX **1871**   * = Microfilm held
Marylebone RD [ff 41-171]*

LONDON/MIDDLESEX **1881**
GSU Transcript & Indexes - county complete [Lower Library]

LONDON MIDDLESEX **1891**
REGISTRATION DISTRICT   RG/12   Location
Bethnal Green RD
 - East SD *part*   267-268   MX/C 17
Whitechapel RD
 - Spitalfields SD *part*   274-275   MX/C 20

NORFOLK (NF)

1570   Norwich paupers survey (NF Rec Soc 40) [NF/PER]
1649   Norwich: Dean & Chapter parliamentary survey (NF Rec Soc 51) [NF/PER]
1767   NF papist return (CRS Occ Paper 2) [RC/PER]

NORFOLK **1841-1881**
Cockley Clay (to 1861 only)   [NF/R 49]
Santon   [NF/R 49]
Stibbard   [NF/ C 1]

NORFOLK **1841**
Norfolk Ancestor, journal of the Norfolk Gen Soc [NFA]
Booton   (NFA 3/7)   [NF/PER]
Colby   (NFA 3/7)   [NF/PER]
Hautbois Magna   (NFA 3/7)   [NF/PER]
Mannington   (NFA 3/7)   [NF/PER]
Oulton (inc workhouse) (NFA 3/7)   [NF/PER]
Saxthorpe   (NFA 3/7)   [NF/PER]
Skeyton   (NFA 3/7)   [NF/PER]
Tuttington   (NFA 3/7)   [NF/PER]
Wickmere   (NFA 3/7)   [NF/PER]
Wolterton   (NFA 3/7)   [NF/PER]

NORFOLK 1851

GSU Pilot Project Transcript & Indexes - county complete [Mfc]   * = Microfilm held

REGISTRATION DISTRICT HO 107		REGISTRATION DISTRICT HO 107	
Aylesham RD	1810*	Kings Lynn RD	1829*
Blofield RD	1819*	Loddon RD	1820*
Depwade RD	1821*	Mitford RD	1824-1825*
Docking RD	1827*	Norwich RD	1812-1816*
Downham RD	1830*	St Faith's RD	1811*
Erpingham RD	1809*	Swaffham RD	1831*
Flegg RD	1807*	Thetford RD	1832*
Forehoe RD	1817*	Tunstead RD	1808*
Freebridge Lynn RD	1828*	Walsingham RD	1826*
Guiltcross RD	1822*	Wayland RD	1823*
Henstead RD	1818*	Yarmouth RD	1806*

NORFOLK 1851

Norfolk Ancestor journal of the Norfolk Gen Soc [NFA]; *Norfolk Genalogy* Norfolk Gen Soc Record Series [NFG]

Aylesham Union	(NFA 3/2)	[NF/PER]
Beckham West Union	(NFA 3/2)	[NF/PER]
Norwich		
- St Edmund	(NFG 9)	[NF/PER]
- St Etheldred	(NFG 9)	[NF/PER]
- St George Colegate	(NFG 9)	[NF/PER]
- St Helen	(NFG 9)	[NF/PER]
- St James	(NFG 9)	[NF/PER]
- St John de Sepulchre		[NF/C 2]
- St Lawrence		[NF/C 2]
- St Martin at Oak	(NFG 7)	[NF/PER]
- St Martin at Place	(NFG 7)	[NF/PER]
- St Michael at Plea	(NFG 9)	[NF/PER]
- St Michael at Thorne		[NF/C 2]
- St Peter Hungate	(NFG 9)	[NF/PER]
- SS Simon & Jude	(NFG 9)	[NF/PER]

NORFOLK 1861

* = Microfilm held

REGISTRATION DISTRICT RG 9		REGISTRATION DISTRICT RG 9	
Aylesham RD	1204-1207	Loddon RD	1228-1230*
Blofield RD	1226-1227*	Mitford RD	1239-1244
Depwade RD	1231-1234*	Norwich RD	1210-1220*
Docking RD	1248-1250*	St Faith's RD	1208-1209
Downham RD	1258-1261	- Sprowston SD	1209*
Erpingham RD	1201-1203*	Swaffham RD	1262-1263
Flegg RD	1195-1196*	Thetford RD	1264-1267*
Forehoe RD	1221-1223*	Tunstead RD	1197-1200*
Freebridge Lynn RD	1251-1254*	Walsingham RD	1245-1247
Guiltcross RD	1235-1236	- Walsingham & Wells SDs	1246-1247*
Henstead RD	1224-1225*	Wayland RD	1237-1238
Kings Lynn RD	1255-1257*	Yarmouth RD	1190-1194

NORFOLK 1891
REGISTRATION DISTRICT   RG 12   Location
Norwich RD (RG 12/1518-1532)
Norwich RD
- Conisford SD *part*   1523   NF/C 5
 (St George Tombland, St Peter per Mountergate,
 St John Timberhill, All Saints, St Michael at Thorn *part*)
- Conisford SD part   1524   NF/C 5
 (St Julian, St Etheldred, St Peter Southgate,
 St John Sepulchre, St Trowse- Millgate, Carrow, Bracondale)
- Mancroft SD *part* (Lakenham)   1525   NF/C 5
- Mancroft SD *part*   1526   NF/C 5
 (Eaton St Andrew, Town, Close)
- Mancroft SD *part*   1527   NF/C 5
 (St Stephen, St Peter Mancroft)
- Norwich West SD *part* (Heigham)   1531   NF/C 5A
- Norwich West SD *part*   1532   Mfc
 (Heigham, Earlham)

NORTHAMPTONSHIRE (NH)

1740-45 Aynho farmers census (Banbury Hist Soc 20) [NH/L 1]
1762 Castor (Inhabitants aged 18-45) (Peterborough & Dist FHS J 2/3)[NH/PER]
1767 NH papist return (CRS Occ Paper 2) [RC/PER]
1790 Aynho householders census (Banbury Hist Soc 20) [NH/L 1]

NORTHAMPTONSHIRE **1841**
Woodford by Thrapston [NH/C 1]

NORTHAMPTONSHIRE **1851**
Northamptonshire FHS 1851 Census Index [NHF]; Huntingdonshire FHS 1851 Census Index [HUF]; Lincolnshire FHS 1851 Census Index [LIF]; Oxfordshire FHS 1851 Census Transcripts & Index [OXF]; Rugby FHS 1851 Census Index [RFG] & GSU Warwickshire 1851 Census Transcript & Index [GSW] .
see also NORTHAMPTONSHIRE FHS 1851 CENSUS INDEXES ARRANGED BY
  HUNDREDS BELOW   * = Microfilm held

REGISTRATION DISTRICT	HO 107	Volume	Location
Brackley RD	1735*		
Brixworth RD	1742*	NHF 6	NH/C 3
Daventry RD	1741*		
- Brockhill, Floore, Whilton & Hardingstone	1741*	NHF 6	NH C/3
Hardingstone RD	1738*		
Kettering RD	1744*		
- Barton Scargrave, Burton Latimer, Cranford & Warkton	1744*	NHF 3	NH/C 3
- Kettering SD	1744*	NHF 4	NH/C 3
- Geddington,Newton, Stanion & Weekly	1744*	NHF 8	NH/C 3
Northampton RD	1739-1740*		
- All Saints & St Sepulchre	1739-40*	NHF 1 & 2	NH/C 3
- Bugbrook, Harpole, Kislingbury, Nether & Upper Heyford, Upton	1740*	NHF 6	NH/C 3

Oundle RD	1746*		
- Deene, Deenthorpe, Great & Little Wheeldon	1746*	NHF 8	NH/C 3
Peterborough RD	1747*	HUF	HU/C 6
Potterspury RD	1737*	HUF	HU/C 6
Thrapston RD	1745*	HUF	HU/C 1
- Brigstock	1745*	NHF 8	NH/C 3
Towcester RD	1736*		
- Abthorpe, Cold Higham, Foscote,Gayton, Pattishall, Tiffield, Towcester	1736*	NHF 7	NH/C 3
Wellingborough RD	1743*		
- Finedon, Isham, Orlingbury	1743*	NHF 3	NH/C 3
- Wellingborough SD	1743*	NFH 5	NH/C 3
Banbury RD - Norhamptonhire part	1734	OXF 9	OX/C 11
Rugby RD - Northamptonshire part	2070	RFG&GSW	Mfc
Stamford RD - Northamptonshire part	2094	LIF 10	LI/C 7

Northamptonshire FHS Microfiche - 1851 census indexes arranged by Hundreds [NUM]

HUNDRED	HO 107	Volume	Location
Higham Ferrers	1743, 1745 parts	NUM 1	Mfc
Fawsley (Parts 1 & 2)	1741, 2070 parts	NUM 2 & 3	Mfc
Rothwell	1742, 1744 & 2079 parts	NUM 4	Mfc
Guilsborough	1741,1742, 2070, 2078 parts	NUM 5	Mfc
Wymersley	1738 part	NUM 6	Mfc

NORTHAMPTONSHIRE 1851 2% Sample [Surname Index] [Mfc]
    Courteenhall; Doddington, Great; Gretton; Hollowell; Raunds; Silverstone

NORTHAMPTONSHIRE 1861   * = Microfilm held

REGISTRATION DISTRICT	RG 9	REGISTRATION DISTRICT	RG 9
Brackley RD	921-923*	Oundle RD	961-963*
Brixworth RD	948-950*	Peterborough RD	964-970
Daventry RD	942-947*	- Crowland & Thorney SDs	968-970*
Hardingstone RD	930-932*	Pottersbury RD	927-929*
Kettering RD	955-958*	Thrapston RD	959-960*
Northampton RD	933-941*	Towcester RD	924-926*
		Wellingborough RD	951-954

NORTHAMPTONSHIRE 1871
Doddington, Great [NH/C 1]

NORTHAMPTONSHIRE 1881
GSU Transcript & Indexes - county complete [Lower Library Mfc]

NORTHUMBERLAND (NU)

1767   NU papist return(CRS Occ Paper 2) [RC/PER]
1781   Backworth census (J NU & DU FHS 17/3) [NU/PER]

NORTHUMBERLAND 1841-1891
Felton & Thirston [NU/C 6]

NORTHUMBERLAND 1851
Northumberland & Durham FHS 1851 Census Index [NUF]   No microfilms held

REGISTRATION DISTRICT	HO 107	Volume	Location
Alnwick RD	2419	NUF 21-23	Mfc
Belford RD	2420(ff1-250)	NUF 18	Mfc
Bellingham RD	2417		
Berwick RD	2421		
- Islandshire SD	2421		
- Tweedmouth SD	2421	NUF 16	Mfc
- Berwick on Tweed SD	2421	NUF 19-20	Mfc
Castle Ward RD	2413		
Glendale RD	2422	NUF 24-25	Mfc
Hexham RD	2414-2415		
Morpeth RD	2418	NUF 1,3-5	NU/C 1
Newcastle on Tyne RD	2404	NUF 10	NU/C 2
Newcastle on Tyne RD	2405	NUF 8	NU/C 2
Newcastle on Tyne RD	2406	NUF 7	NU/C 2
Newcastle on Tyne RD	2407	NUF 11	NU/C 2
Newcastle on Tyne RD	2408	NUF 12	NU/C 2
Rothbury RD	2423(ff1-117)	NUF 17	Mfc
Tynemouth RD	2409	NUF 13-15	Mfc
Tynemouth RD	2410(ff1-233)	NUF 6	NU/C 1
- Cullercoats & Whitley Bay	2410(ff237-499)	NUF 26	Mfc
Tynemouth RD	2411(ff1-288)	NUF 9	NU/C 2
Tynemouth RD	2412(ff1-153)	NUF 2	NU/C 1

NORTHUMBERLAND 1851 2% Sample [surname index] [Mfc]
Bullocks Hall; Cambo; Dalton; Doddington; Feathersone; Lemmington; Newton Hall; Prestwick; Sunderland, North; Tosson, Little

NORTHUMBERLAND 1861
Northern Forebears census indxes [NFB]   No microfilms held

REGISTRATION DISTRICT	RG 9	Volume	Location
Castleward RD			
- Stamfordham SD	3854-3855	NFB 1	Mfc
Hexham RD			
- Hexham SD	3858-3860	NFB 2`	Mfc
- Bywell SD	3856-3857	NFB 3	Mfc

NORTHUMBERLAND 1871

REGISTRATION DISTRICT	RG 10	Location
Newcastle on Tyne RD	(NB. 5093 not used)	
- Westgate SD	5069-5075	Mfc
- ElswicK SD	5076-5082	Mfc
- St Andrew SD	5085-5089	Mfc
- SS Nicholas & John SDs	5090-5092	Mfc
- All Saints SD	5094-5102	Mfc
- St Anne's Chapelry & St Anthony's Byker SD	5103-5105	Mfc

NORTHUMBERLAND 1881
GSU Transcripts & Indexes - county complete [Lower Library Mfc]

NORTHUMBERLAND **1891**
Berwick RO index
Berwick [Mfc]

NOTTINGHAMSHIRE (NT)

1676 Clayworth census (NT FHS Rec Ser 99) [NT/PER]
1688 Clayworth census (NT FHS Rec Ser 99) [NT/PER]
1696 Hucknall Torkard census (NT FHS Rec Ser 105) [NT/PER]
1767 NT papist return (CRS Occ Paper 2) [RC/PER]
1787 Wollaton census (NT FHS Rec Ser 88) [Apply to Staff (Shelf 9)]
1794 West Retford census (NT FHS Rec Ser 105) [NT/PER]
1801 Eakring, Kinoulton & Welbeck Abbey censuses (NT FHS Rec Ser 95) [NT/PER]
1803 Norwell census (NT FHS Rec Ser 105) [NT/PER]
1811 Gotham, Kinoulton, Laxton, West Retford & Worksop censuses (NT FHS Rec Ser 95) [NT/PER]
1815 Bilborough & Strelley census (NT FHS Rec Ser 105) [NT/PER]
1818 Strelley census (NT FHS Rec Ser 105) [NT/PER]
1821 Gamston, Gotham, Kinoulton, Laxton, Radford, Syerston & Thorpe next Newark censuses (NT FHS Rec Ser 95) [NT/PER]
1828 East Stoke census (NT FHS Rec Ser 105) [NT/PER]
1831 Beckingham, Blyth, Car Colston, Edwalton, Gotham, Mansfield, Torworth & Walkeringham censuses (NT FHS Rec Ser 95) [NT/PER]; Mansfield census [NT/L 39]
1832 Barnby Moor census (NT FHS Rec Ser 109)[NT/PER]
1845 Carlton upon Trent census (NT FHS Rec Ser 105) [NT/PER]
1846 Caunton census (NT FHFS Rec Ser 109) [NT/PER]
1878 Farnsfield census (NT FHS Rec Ser 99) [NT/PER]

NOTTINGHAMSHIRE **1841**
Nottinghamshire FHS 1841 Census Index [NTF]
Please note Registration Districts were not used in this county in 1841.
A full guide to the indexes covering each parish appears in NTF 96 - county complete.
Surname Index   HO 107/849-863, 865-871   NT/C 8 & Mfc
Place Name Index   NTF 96   NT/C 8

The 1841 districts were based on Wapentakes.
The Society holds microfilms for the following Hundreds/Wapentakes:

DISTRICT/HUNDRED	HO 107	DISTRICT/HUNDRED	HO 107
Bassetlaw	850-852	Thurgarten	865-867
Bingham/Broxtow	852-855	Newark on Trent	868
Broxtow	856-860	Nottingham St Mary	869-870
Rushcliffe	863		

NOTTINGHAMSHIRE**1851**
Nottinghamshire FHS 1851 Census Index [NTF]
Place Name Index   NTF 96 [NT/C 8]   * = Microfilm held

REGISTRATION DISTRICT	HO 107	Volume	Location
Basford RD	2125-2128*	NTF 7/1	NT/C 1-2
BinghamRD	2139*	NTF 4	NT/C 1-2
East Retford RD	2121*	NTF 8	NT/C 1-2
Mansfield RD	2123-2124*	NTF 3	NT/C 1-2
Newark RD	2136-2138*	NTF 5	NT/C 1-2

Nottingham RD	2131-2133	NTF 10	NT/C 1-2 & Mfc
Radford RD	2129-2130*	NTF 16	NT/C 1-2
Southwell RD	2134-2135*	NTF 14	NT/C 1-2
Worksop RD	2122	NTF 9	NT/C 1-2
Doncaster RD - Nottinghamshire part	2438	NTF 9	NT/C 1-2
Gainsborough RD - Notts. part	2119*	NTF 9	NT/C 1-2
Loughborough RD - Notts. part	2086*	NTF 7	NT/C 1-2
Melton Mowbray RD -Notts. part	2091*	NTF 4	NT/C 1-2
Shardlow RD - Nottinghamshire part	2140-2141	NTF7	NT/C 1-2

NOTTINGHAMSHIRE 1861
Nottinghamshire FHS 1861 Census Index [NTF]
Place Name Index   NTF 96 [NT/C 8]   * = Microfilm held

REGISTRATION DISTRICT	RG 9	Volume	Location
Basford RD	2431-2446*	NTF 55/1	NT/C 5
Bingham RD	2483-2486*	NTF 55/2	NT/C 5
East Retford RD	2412-2417*	NTF 42	NT/C 5
Mansfield RD	2423-2430*	NTF 46	NT/C 5
Newark RD	2476-2482*	NTF 58	NT/C 5
Nottingham RD	2453-2469*	NTF 48/1-2	NT/C 5
Radford RD	2447-2452*	NTF 60	NT/C 5
Southwell RD	2470-2475*	NTF 58	NT/C 5
Worksop RD	2418-2422*	NTF 41	NT/C 5
Doncaster RD - Nottinghamshire part	3522*	NTF 41	NT/C 5
Gainsborough RD -Notts. part	2407	NTF 41	NT/C 5
Loughborough RD -Notts. part	2277-2278*	NTF 55/2	NT/C 5
Melton Mowbray RD - Notts. part	2301*	NTF 55/2	NT/C 5
Shardlow RD - Nottinghamshire part	2488, 2491-2492	NTF 55/2	NT/C 5

Passengers & crew on ships in port and at sea - extract, people born in Nottinghamshire
(NT FHS Rec Ser 99) [NT/PER]

NOTTINGHAMSHIRE 1871
Nottinghamshire FHS 1871 Census Index [NTF]
Place Name Index   NTF 96 [NT/C 8]

REGISTRATION DISTRICT	RG 10	Volume	Location
Basford RD	3476-3498	NTF 71/1-2	NT/C 7
Bingham RD	3546-3549	NTF 80	NT/C 7
East Retford RD	3450-3457	NTF 67	NT/C 7
Mansfield RD	3464-3475	NTF 76	NT/C 7
Newark RD	3539-3545	NTF 79	NT/C 7
Nottingham RD	3506-3531	NTF 62/1-2	NT/C 7
Radford RD	3499-3505	NTF 64	NT/C 7
Southwell RD	3532-3538	NTF 32	NT/C 7
Worksop RD	3458-3483	NTF 68	NT/C 7
Doncaster RD- Nottinghamshire part	4723	NTF 67	NT/C 7
Gainsborough RD -Notts. part	3443	NTF 67	NT/C 7
Loughborough RD -Notts. part	3259-3260	NTF 80	NT/C 7
Melton Mowbray RD - Notts. part	3296	NTF 80	NT/C 7
Shardlow RD - Nottinghamshire part	3550, 3554-3555	NTF 80	NT/C 7

NOTTINGHAMSHIRE 1881
GSU Transcripts & Indexes - county complete [Lower Library]

Nottinghamshire FHS 1881 Census Index [NTF]
Place Name index   NTF 96 [NT/C 8]

REGISTRATION DISTRICT	RG 11	Volume	Location
Basford RD	3320-3339	NTF 29/1-3	NT/C 3-4
Bingham RD	3380-3383	NTF 29/3	NT/C 3-4
East Retford RD	3299-3304	NTF 37	NT/C 3-4
Mansfield RD	3311-3319	NTF 35	NT/C 3-4
Newark RD	3373-3379	NTF 32	NT/C 3-4
Nottingham RD	3349-3367	NTF 22/1-3	NT/C 3-4
Radford RD	3340-3348	NTF 26	NT/C 3-4
Southwell RD	3368-3372	NTF 32	NT/C 3-4
Worksop RD	3305-3310	NTF 28	NT/C 3-4
Doncaster RD - Nottinghamshire part	4695	NTF 37	NT/C 3-4
Gainsborough RD - Notts. part	3294	NTF 37	NT/C 3-4
Loughborough RD -Notts. part	3148-3149	NTF 29/3	NT/C 3-4
Melton Mowbray RD -Notts. part	3184	NTF 29/3	NT/C 3-4
Shardlow RD - Nottinghamshire part	3389, 3391	NTF 29/2	NT/C 3-4

"At Sea" extract - List of Nottinghamshire persons serving in the Royal Navy (NT FHS Rec Ser 99) [NT/PER]

NOTTINGHAMSHIRE 1891
Nottinghamshire FHS 1891 Census Index [NTF]
Place Name Index   NTF 96 [NT/C 8]

REGISTRATION DISTRICT	RG 12	Volume	Location
Basford RD	2658-2680	NTF 85/4	NT/C 9
Bingham RD	2717-2718	NTF 85/8	NT/C 9
East Retford RD	2638-2642	NTF 85/6	NT/C 9
Mansfield RD	2648-2657	NTF 85/7	NT/C 9
Newark RD	2711-2716	NTF 85/5	NT/C 9
Nottingham RD	2681-2706	NTF 85/1-2	NT/C 9
Radford RD	now part of Nottingham RD		
Southwell RD	2707-2710	NTF 85/5	NT/C 9
Worksop RD	2643-2647	NTF 85/6	NT/C 9
Doncaster RD - Nottinghamshire part	3867	NTF 85/6	NT/C 9
Gainsborough RD - Notts. part	2633	NTF 85/6	NT/C 9
Loughborough RD - Notts. part	2518	NTF 85/8	NT/C 9
Melton Mowbray RD - Notts. part	2545	NTF 85/8	NT/C 9
Shardlow RD - Nottinghamshire part	2719, 2723-2725	NTF 85/8	NT/C 9

OXFORDSHIRE (OX)

1642-46   Oxford City strangers [OX/L 35]
1767   OX papist return (CRS Occ Paper 2) [RC/PER]
1801   Stoke Lyne census (OX FHn 1/9) [OX/PER]
1821   Caversham census [Apply to Staff (SP 54/ 30)]
            Wolvercote census (OS FHn 3/3) [OX/PER]
1832   Oxford: Summertown list extract (Loc Population Studies 28) [PER/LOC]

OXFORDSHIRE **1841**
Oxfordshire FHS 1841 Census Index [OXF]
REGISTRATION DISTRICT HO 107 Location
Abingdon Union - Oxfordshire part 0020, 0024, 0032 Mfc
Walllingford Union - Oxfordshire part 0023, 0030, 0025 Mfc

The 1841 districts were based upon the Hundreds.
The Society has microfilms for the following Hundreds:

DISTRICT/HUNDRED	HO 107	DISTRICT/HUNDRED	HO 107
Chadlington/Dorchester	0878-0880	Ploughley/Thame	0885-0888
Ewelme/Langtree	0881-0882	Wooton	0889-0890
Lewknor/Pirton	0883-0884		

OXFORDSHIRE **1851**
Oxfordshire FHS 1851 Census Transcripts & Index [OXF]
A complete index for the county is held on computer. Apply to staff
Name Indexes [OX/C 1] * = Microfilm held

REGISTRATION DISTRICT	HO 107	Volume	Location
Banbury RD	1733-1734*	OXF 9	OX/C 10-11
Bicester RD	1729*	OXF 5	OX/C 6
Chipping Norton RD	1732*	OXF 8	OX/C 9
Headington RD	1727*	OXF 4	OX/C 5
Henley RD	1725*	OXF 1	OX/C 2
Oxford RD	1728*	OXF 12	OX/C 14
Thame RD	1726*	OXF 2	OX/C 3
Witney RD	1731*	OXF 7	OX/C 8
Woodstock RD	1730*	OXF 6	OX/C 7
Abingdon RD - Oxfordshire part	1688*	OXF 10	OX/C 12
Brackley RD - Oxfordshire part	1735*	OXF 11	OX/C 13
Bradfield RD - Oxfordshire part	1691*	OXF 11	OX/C 13
Farringdon RD - Oxfordshire part	1687*	OXF 7	OX/C 7
Wallingford RD - Oxfordshire part	1690*	OXF 3	OX/C 3
Wycombe RD - Oxfordshire part	1720	OXF 11	OX/C 13

OXFORDSHIRE **1861** * = Microfilm held

REGISTRATION DISTRICT	RG 9
Banbury RD	913-920*
Bicester RD	897-900*
Chipping Norton RD	909-912*
Headington RD	889-892*
Henley RD	880-884
Oxford RD	893-396*
Thame RD	885-888*
Witney RD	904-908*
Woodstock RD	902-902* (903 has not survived)
Abingdon RD - Oxfordshire part	730-735*
Farringdon RD - Oxfordshire part	727-729*
Wallingford RD - Oxfordshire part	739-741*

OXFORDSHIRE **1871**
Oxfordshire FHS 1871 Census Index

REGISTRATION DISTRICT	RG 10	Location
Bicester RD	1442-1445	Mfc
Chipping Norton RD	1455-1458	Mfc
Headington RD - Wheatley & Oxford St Clements SDs	1434-1436	Mfc
Henley RD	1425-1427	Mfc
Oxford City RD	1437-1440,1771	Mfc
Thame RD	1429-1432	Mfc
Abingdon RD - Oxfordshire part	1261-1266	Mfc
Wallingford RD - Oxfordshire part	1272-1274	Mfc

OXFORDSHIRE **1881**
GSU Transcript & Indexes - county complete [Lower Library Mfc]

OXFORDSHIRE **1891**
Oxfordshire FHS 1891 Census Index: County Complete

REGISTRATION DISTRICT	RG 12	Location
Banbury RD	1180-1184	Mfc
Bicester RD	1170-1171	Mfc
Chipping Norton RD	1178-1179	Mfc
Headington RD	1162-1166	Mfc
Henley RD	1156-1159	Mfc
Oxford RD	1167-1169	Mfc
Thame RD	1160-1161	Mfc
Witney RD	1174-1177	Mfc
Woodstock RD	1172-1173	Mfc
Abingdon RD - Oxfordshire part	0977-0981	Mfc
Brackley RD - Oxfordshire part	1186	Mfc
Bradfield RD - Oxfordshire part	0988-0990	Mfc
Farringdon RD - Oxfordshire part	0974-0976	Mfc
Wallingford RD - Oxfordshire part	0985-0986	Mfc
Wantage RD - Oxfordshire part	0982-0984	Mfc
Wycombe RD - Oxfordshire part	1159	Mfc

RUTLAND (RU)

1767   RU papist return (CRS Occ Paper 2) [RC/PER]

RUTLAND **1851**
Leicestershire FHS 1851 Census Index of Rutland [RU] & Lincolnshire FHS 1851 Census Index [LIF]

REGISTRATION DISTRICT	HO 107	Volume	Location
Oakham RD	2092*	RU 1	RU/C 1
Uppingham RD	2093*		
Stamford RD - Rutland part	2094*	LIF 10	LI/C 2-3

RUTLAND **1861**

REGISTRATION DISTRICT	RG 9	* = Microfilm held
Oakham RD	2305-2307*	
Uppingham RD	2308-2310	

SHROPSHIRE (SH)

1767 SH papist return (CRS Occ Paper 2) [RC/PER]
1821 Wellington census [SH/C 8]
1831 Bishops Castle census [SH/C 7]

SHROPSHIRE **1841**   No microfilms held
Bishops Castle [SH/C9]   Newport [SH/C 7]
Myddle [SH/C 7]   Wellington [SH/C 7]

SHROPSHIRE **1851**   * = Microfilm held
REGISTRATION DISTRICT HO 107   REGISTRATION DISTRICT HO 107
Atcham RD   1990-1991*   Market Drayton RD   1996*
Bridgenorth RD   1986*   Newport RD   1998*
Church Stretton RD   1984*   Oswestry RD   1993*
Cleobury Mortimer RD   1985*   Shifnal RD   1987*
Clun RD   1983*   Shrewsbury RD   1992*
Ellesmere RD   1994*   Wellington RD   1997*
Ludlow RD   1982*   Wem RD   1995*
Madeley RD   1988-1989*

Shropshire FHS 1851 parish indexes [C-x] and
Herefordsire FHS 1851 Census Index - Tenbury RD [HET]

Acton Burnell C-3	Bloore C-6	Culmington C-1
Acton Bound C-1	Boningale C-3	Dawley, Great C-2
Acton Scott C-1	Boscobel C-3	Diddlebury C-1
Adderley C-6	Bromfield C-2	Ditton Priors C-1
Alberbury C-1	Bucknall C-1	Donington C-3
Albrighton near	Bucknell C-2	Dorrington C-6
Shrewsbury C-6	Burford HET Mfc	Drayton Magna C-6
Albrighton near	Buildwas C-1	Drayton Parva C-6
Wolverhampton C-6	Cardington C-6	Easthope C-1
Alveley C-2	Cardiston C-1 & 6	Eaton C-6
Ashford Bowdler C-2	Caynham C-3	Eaton Constantine C-6
Ashford Carbonell C-3	Cheswadine /6	Eaton under Heywood C-1
Astley C-6	Childs Ercall C-6	Edgton C-2 & 3
Aston Botterell C-2	Chipnall C-6	Ellerton C-6
Aston Eyre C-1	Chirbury C-1	Farlow C-2
Atcham C-6	Church Preen C-3	Fitz C-3
Badger C-3	Church Pulverbatch C-1	Ford C-2
Barrow C-3	Church Stretton C-1	Frodesley C-3
Baschurch C-3	Clee Downton C-1	Goldstone C-6
Battlefield C-6	Clee Saint Margaret C-1	Gravenhunger C-6
Bearstone C-6	Clee Stanton C-1	Greet C-2 & HET Mfc
Beckbury C-6	Cleobury Mortimer C-3	Habberley C-1
Bedstone C-2	Cleobury North C-2	Halford C-1
Benthall C-3	Clun C-1	Hanwood, Great C-3
Berrington C-3	Clunbury C-1	Harley C-2 & 3
Betton C-6	Clungunford C-1	Haughmond Demesne C-6
Bishops Castle C-1	Condover C-1	Hawkestone C-6
Bitterley C-3	Cound C-2	Heath C-1
Bletchley C-6	Cressage C-2	Highley C-2

53

Hinstock C-6
Hodnet C-6
Holdgate C-3
Hope Baggott C-2
Hope Bowdler C-3
Hopesay C-1
Hopton C-6
Hopton Cangeford C-3
Hopton Castle C-2
Hughley C-3
Kemberton C-3
Kenley C-2
Kenstone C-6
Kinlet C-3
Knockin C-2
Langley C-4
Leebotwood C-1
Leighton C-6
Linley C-3
Llanfair Waterdine C-2
Llanymynech C-3
Longford C-6
Longnor C-3
Longslow C-6
Lostford C-6
Loughton C-2
Ludford C-2
Ludlow C-2
Lydbury , North C-1 & 3
Lydham C-3
Mainstone C-3
Marchamley C-6
Melverley C-3
Milson C-2
Mindtown C-1
Minstereley C-1
Monkhopton C-1
Montford C-4
More C-1
Moreton Saye C-6

Morville C-1
Munslow C-1
Myddle C-1 & 2
Neen Savage C-2
Neen Sollars C-2
Ness, Great C-2
Newport C-4
Norbury C-4
Norncott, Lower C-1
Norncott, Upper C-6
Norton in Hales C-6
Ollerton C-6
Onibury C-1
Oswestry C-4
Peplow C-6
Petton C-3
Pitchford C-4
Pontesbury C-1
Posenhall C-4
Preston Gubbals
Ratlinghope C-1
Richards Castle C-2
Rushbury C-1
Ryton C-4
St Martin C-4
Sambrook C-6
Selattyn C-2
Shawbury C-1
Sheinton C-4
Shelve C-4
Sheriff Hales C-4
Shifnal C-1
Shipton C-1
Shrawardine C-2
Shrewsbury C-1
Sibdon Carwood C-1
Silvington C-2
Smethcote C-1
Sowdley C-6
Stanton Lacey C-1

Stanton Long C-1
Stapleton C-1
Stirchley C-4
Stockton C-4
Stoke Saint Milborough C-1
Stokesay C-1
Stoke upon Tern C-6
Stottesdon C-2
Stowe C-2
Styche C-6
Sutton C-4
Sutton Maddock C-4
Tittenley C-6
Tong C-4
Tugford C-1
Tyrley Quarter C-6
Uffington C-6
Uppington C-6
Upton Cressett C-1
Upton Magna C-6
Wellington C-10
Wem Union Workhouse C-6
Wenlock, Little C-4
Wenlock, Much C-4
Wentnor C-1
Westbury C-1
Wheathill C-2
Whittington C-4
Willey C-3
Wistanstow C-6
Wistanwick C-1
Withington C-6
Wollerton C-6
Woodlands C-6
Woodseaves C-6
Woolstaston C-4
Woore C-6
Worthen C-6
Wroxeter C-6

SHROPSHIRE **1861**   * = Microfilm held
Bishops Castle [C-6];   Myddle [C-7]; Shrewsbury [C-6]

REGISTRATION DISTRICT	RG 9	REGISTRATION DISTRICT	RG 9
Atcham RD	1861-1868	**Market Drayton RD**	1892-1895
Bridgenorth RD	1848-1851*	- Hodnet SD	1895*
Church Stretton RD	1844-1845*	**Newport RD**	1901-1904*
Cleobury Mortimer RD	1846-1847*	**Oswestry RD**	1875-1879*
Clun RD	1840-1843*	**Shifnal RD**	1852-1854*
Ellesmere RD	1881-1885	**Shrewsbury RD**	1869-1874*
Ludlow RD	1834-1839*	**Wellington RD**	1869-1900*
Madeley RD	1855-1860*	**Wem RD**	1886-1888

SHROPSHIRE **1881**
GSU Transcript & Indexes - county complete [Lower Library]

SOMERSET (SO)

1767 SO papist return (CRS Occ Paper 2) [RC/PER]
1811 High Littleton & Hallatrow census [SO/C 11]

SOMERSET 1841
Frome [SO/C 1]

The 1841 districts were based upon the Hundreds.
The Society has microfilms for the following Hundreds:

DISTRICT/HUNDRED	HO 107
Glaston-Twelve-Hides/Hampton & Claverton/Hartcliffe & Bedminster & Horethorne	0943-0945
East & West Kingsbury *parts*	0949-0950

SOMERSET 1851   * = Microfilm held
Somerset & Dorset FHS 1851 Census Index Vols 1-7, includes Master Surname Index [SOF];
Bristol & Avon FHS 1851 Census Index [BAF];
Devon FHS 1851 Census Index [DEF];
GSU Devon 1851 Transript & Indexes including cross county districts [GSD]. County complete.

REGISTRATION DISTRICT	HO 107	Volume	Location
Axbridge RD	1936-1937*	SOF 7 & BAF	SO/C 2 & Mfc
Bath RD	1940-1943	BAF 9-15	SO/C 9-10
- Twerton/Bathwick SDs	1940	BAF 9-10	SO/C 10
- Abbey SD	1941	BAF 11	SO/C 9
- Lynchcombe & Walcot SDs	1942	BAF 12-13	SO/C 10
- Landsdown & Batheaton SDs	1943	BAF 14-15	SO/C 10
Bedminster RD	1945	BAF 7	SO/C 9
Bedminster RD	1946	BAF 16	Mfc
Bridgewater RD	1924-1925	SOF 2, 3	SO/C 2
Chard RD	1927	DEF36, GSD	DE/C 6 & Mfc
Chard RD	1927-1928	SOF 3, 4	SO/C 2
Clutton RD	1938-1939	BAF 16	Mfc
Frome RD	1932	SOF 5	SO/C 2
Keynsham RD - Newton & Keynsham SDs Somerset part	1944 ff489-end	BAF 16	Mfc
Langport RD	1926	SOF 3	SO/C 2
Shepton Mallet RD	1933	SOF 6	SO/C 2
Taunton RD	1922-1923	SOF 2	SO/C 2
Wellington RD - Somerset part	1921ff 311-end	SOF 1,DEF 39	SO/C 2 & DE/C 6
Wells RD			
- Wells SD	1934	SOF 6	SO/C 2
- Glastonbury SD	1935*	SOF 7	SO/C2
Williton RD	1920	SOF 1	SO/C 2
Wincanton RD	1931	SOF 5	SO/C 2
Yeovil RD	1929-1930*	SOF 4	SO/C 2
Tiverton RD			
- Dulverton SD Somerset part	1890*	DEF 24,GSD	DE/C5 & Mfc

SOMERSET 1861   * = Microfilm held
Bedminster [SO/C 9]
REGISTRATION DISTRICT   RG 9   REGISTRATION DISTRICT   RG 9
Axbridge RD   1668-1676*   Langport RD   1628-1632*
Bath RD   1682-1697   Shepton Mallet RD   1658-1662*
Bedminster RD   1703-1711*   Taunton RD   1613-1620*
Bridgewater RD   1621-1627*   Wellington RD   1608-1612*
Chard RD   1633-1638*   Wells RD   1663-1667*
Clutton RD   1677-1681*   Williton RD   1601-1605*
Dulverton RD   1606-1607*   Wincanton RD   1646-1645*
Frome RD   1652-1657*   Yeovil RD   1639-1645*
Keynsham RD   1698-1702*

SOMERSET 1871
Weston Super Mare - extracts of resident born in Bristol [SO/C 9]

SOMERSET 1881
GSU Transcript & indexes - county complete [Lower Library Mfc]

SOMERSET 1891
Weston Super Mare FHS 1891 surname indexes [WSF]
REGISTRATION DISTRICT   RG 12   Volume   Location
Axbridge RD
 - Axbridge SD   1992   WSF1   SO/C 12
 - Blagdon SD   1923   WSF2   SO/C 12
 - Burnham SD   1918   WSF3   SO/C 12
 - Weston Super Mare SD   1919-1921   WSF 4-5   SO/C 12
Bedminster RD
 - Long Ashton SD   1953   WSF 6   SO/C 13
 - St George SD   1956   WSF 7   SO/C 13
 - Yatton SD   1955   WSF 8   SO/C 13

STAFFORDSHIRE (ST)

1767   ST papist return (CRS Occ Paper 2) [RC/PER]

STAFFORDSHIRE 1841
Burton on Trent [SP 58/18]
The 1841 Districts were based upon the Hundreds.
The Society holds microfilms for the following Hundreds:
DISTRICT/HUNDRED   HO 107
South Offlow *part*   980-982, 984
North Seisdon   996-998

STAFFORDSHIRE 1851   * = Microfilm held
Birmingham & Midland SGH 1851 Census Index of Staffordshire [STB];
Birmingham & Midland SGH 1851 Census Index of Worcestershire [WOB]
REGISTRATION DISTRICT   HO 107   Volume   Location
Burton on Trent RD   2011-2012*   STB 9   ST/C 14
Cheadle RD   2009*
Dudley RD
 - Rowley Regis SD   2028*
 - Tipton SD   2029*

56

- Sedgley SD	2030-2031*		
- Dudley SD	2032-2033*		
Leek RD	2008*		
Lichfield RD	2014-2015*	STB 11	Mfc
Newcastle under Lyme RD	2001*		
Penkridge RD	2016*	STB 12	ST/C 14
Stafford RD	1999*	STB 1 & 2	ST/C 2
Stoke on Trent RD			
- Henley/Shelton SDs	2004-2005	STB 5	ST/C 2
- Stoke on Trent & Fenton/			
Longton SDs	2006-2007*		
Stone RD	2000*	STB 1 & 2	ST/C 2
Tamworth RD	2013*		
Uttoxeter RD	2010*		
Walsall RD	2022-2023*		
West Bromwich RD			
- Handsworth & Oldbury SDs	2024*	STB 15 pt 1	ST/C 15
- West Bromwich SD	2025	STB 15 pt 1	ST/C 15
- West Bromwich SD	2026	STB 15 pt 2	ST/C 15
- Wednesbury SD	2027*	STB 15 pt 2	ST/C 15
Wolstanton RD	2002-2003*	STB 4	ST/C 2
Wolverhampton RD			
- Tetttenhall/Kinfare/Womburn SDs	2017*		
- Wolverhampton Western SD	2018*		
- Wolverhampton Eastern SD	2019*	STB 13	ST/C 14
- Willenhall SD	2020*		
- Bilston SD	2021*		
Kings Norton RD - Harborn SD	2050*	STB	Mfc
Newport RD - Staffordshire part	1998	STB 1 & 2	ST/C 2
Shifnal RD - Staffordshire part	1987	STB 1 & 2	ST/C 2
Stourbridge RD - Kings Swinford SD	2036	WOB 1	ST/C 1

STAFFORDSHIRE **1851**
Shropshire FHS indexes for the following parishes :
Ashley; Aston; Knighton; Muckleston; Oakley; Winnington [SH/C 6]

STAFFORDSHIRE **1851** 2% Sample [Surname Index] [Mfc]
   Butterton; Handford; Hilton; Oakley; Ranton; Streethay; Warley Wighorn

STAFFORDSHIRE **1861**   * = Microfilm held

REGISTRATION DISTRICT	**RG 9**	**REGISTRATION DISTRICT**	**RG 9**
Burton on Trent RD	1957-1967*	**Stone RD**	1910-1914
Cheadle RD	1950-1953	- Stone & Eccleshall SDs	1810-1913*
Dudley RD	2037-2058*	**Tamworth RD**	1968-1971*
Leek RD	1945-1949	**Uttoxeter RD**	1955-1957*
Lichfield RD	1972-1978*	**Walsall RD**	2009-2018*
Newcastle under Lyme RD	1915-1920	**West Bromwich RD**	2019-2036*
Penkridge RD	1979-1983*	**Wolstanton RD**	1921-1930
Stafford RD	1905-1909*	**Wolverhampton RD**	1984-2008*
Stoke on Trent RD	1931-1944		

STAFFORDSHIRE **1881**
GSU Transcript & Indexes - county complete [Lower Library Mfc]

STAFFORDSHIRE **1891**
Cheshire 1891 Census index (CHC)
Congleton RD - Biddulph (CHC) [Mfc]

SUFFOLK (SF)

1767 SF papist return (CRS Occ Paper 2) [RC/PER]

SUFFOLK **1841**
The 1841 districts were based upon the Hundreds.
The Society has microfilms for the following Hundreds:

DISTRICT/HUNDRED	HO 107	DISTRICT/HUNDRED	HO 107
Babergh/ Blackbourn	1012-1013	Plomesgate	1031-1042
Blackbourn/Blything	1014-1016	Risbridge/Samford	1033-1034
Hertismere/Hoxne	1024-1026	Stow/Thedwestry	1035-1036
Lackford/Loes	1027-1028	Wilford/Bury St Edmunds	1041-1042

SUFFOLK **1851**
Suffolk FHS 1851 Census Index [SUF], GSU pilot project 1851 **Norfolk** transcripts & indexes including cross county districts [GSN]   * = Microfilm held

REGISTRATION DISTRICT	HO 107	Volume	Location
Blything RD	1903*		
Bosmere RD	1797*	SUF 12	SF/C 5
Bury St Edmunds RD	1792*	SUF 6	SF/C 3
Cosford RD	1790*	SUF 4	SF/C 2
Hartismere RD	1795*	SUF 10	SF/C 4
Hoxne RD	1796*	SUF 11	SF/C 4
Ipswich RD	1799-1800*	SUF 14	SF/C 6
Mildenhall RD	1793*	SUF 7	SF/C 3
Mutford RD	1805*		
Plomesgate RD	1802*		
Risbridge RD	1787*	SUF 1	SF/C 1
Samford RD	1798*	SUF 13	SF/C 5
Stow RD	1794*		
Sudbury RD			
- Bulmer/Bures SDs	1788*	SUF 2	SF/C 1
- Sudbury/MelfordSDs	1789*	SUF 3	SF/C 1
Thingoe RD	1791*	SUF 5	SF/C 2
Wangford RD	1804*		
Woodbridge RD	1801*	SUF 15	SF/C 7
Thetford RD - Suffolk part	1832*	SUF 9& GSN	SF/C 4 & Mfc

SUFFOLK **1851 2% Sample** [Surname Index] [Mfc]
   Barking; Braiseworth; Burgh; Cockfield; Denston; Ellough; Horningheath; Huntingfield; Stowlangtoft; Wickham Market

SUFFOLK 1861   * = Microfilm held

REGISTRATION DISTRICT	RG 9	REGISTRATION DISTRICT	RG 9
Blything RD	1178-1183*	Plomesgate RD	1172-1177*
Bosmere RD	1155-1158*	Risbridge RD	1124-1216*
Bury St Edmunds RD	1140-1141*	Samford RD	1159-1160*
Cosford RD	1133-1136*	Stow RD	1144-1147*
Hartismere RD	1148-1154*	Sudbury RD	1127-1132*
Hoxne RD	1151-1154*	Thingoe RD	1137-1139*
Ipswich RD	1161-1166*	Wangford RD	1184-1185*
Mildenhall RD	1142-1143*	Woodbridge RD	1167-1171*
Mutford RD	1186-1189*	Thetford RD - Suffolk part	1264-1267*

SUFFOLK 1871
Suffolk Immigrants to Cleveland [YK/C 16]

SUFFOLK 1881
GSU Transcript & Indexes - county complete [Lower Library Mfc]

SURREY (SR)

1767   SR papist return (CRS Occ Paper 2) [RC/PER]

SURREY 1801
Chobham (Root & Branch 13/4-14/1) [SR/PER]
Clapham [SR/C 10]
Ewhhurst (Root & Branch 12/2) [SR/PER] & [SR/C 10]
Guildford [SR/C 10]
Newdigate (Root & Branch 6/3) [SR/PER]

SURREY 1811
Chobham cen (Root & Branch 23/1) [SR/PER]
Clapham [SR/C 10]
Croydon census (Mfc) [Apply to Staff (with Apprentice Regs 1803-04) & [SR/C 10]
Mitcham [SR/C 10]

SURREY 1821
Clapham [SR/C 10]

SURREY 1841
Leatherhead [SR/C 10]
Wallington [SR/C 2]
London Metropolitan area street index [Mfc]

The 1841 districts were based upon the Hundreds.
The Society has microfilms for the following Hundreds:

DISTRICT/HUNDRED	HO 107	DISTRICT/HUNDRED	HO 107
Brixton	1050-1069	Kingston/Reigate	1075-1076
Brixton/Copthorn	1069-1070	Tandridge	1077
Godalming	1073	Wallington	1078
Godley	1074	Wotton/Guildford	1081-1082
Kingston	1075	Southwark	1083-1088

SURREY **1851**   * = Microfilm held
West Surrey FHS 1851 Census Index [WSR]; East Surrey FHS 1851 Census Index [ESR].
See also map showing Greater London RDs from staff at Middle Library Enquiry Counter

REGISTRATION DISTRICT	HO 107	Volume	Location
Bermondsey RD	1560-1562*		
Camberwell RD	1580-1582*	WSR 9	Mfc Shelf 9
Chertsey RD	1593*	WSR 1	Mfc Shelf 9
Croydon RD	1601-1602*	ESR 3-5 & 11	SR/C 16 & Mfc
Dorking RD	1598*	WSR 1	Mfc Shelf 9
Epsom RD			
- Carshalton SD	1592*	ESR 2	SR/C 16
- Epsom SD	1592*	ESR 2 pt 2	Mfc Shelf 9
- Leatherhead parish	1592*	ESR 2 pt 3	Mfc Shelf 9
- Leatherhead SD Surrey part	1592*	WSR 1	Mfc shelf 9
Farnborough RD	1596*	WSR 1	Mfc Shelf 9
Farnham RD	1595*	WSR 1	Mfc Shelf 9
Godstone RD	1600*	ESR 1	SR/C 16
Guildford RD	1594*	WSR 1	Mfc Shelf 9
Hambledon RD	1597*	WSR 1	Mfc Shelf 9
Kingston RD	1603-1604*	ESR 7	Mfc Shelf 9
- Esher SD	1604*	WSR 1	Mfc Shelf 9
Lambeth RD	1569-1575*		
- Waterloo Road SD	1569-1570*	ESR 9 pt 4	Mfc Shelf 9
- Lambeth Church SD	1571-1572*	ESR 9 pt 1	Mfc Shelf 9
- Kennington SD	1573-1574*	ESR 9 pt 2	Mfc Shelf 9
- Brixton & Norwood SDs	1575*	ESR 9 pt 3	Mfc Shelf 9
Newington RD	1566-1568*		
Reigate RD	1599*	ESR 8	Mfc Shelf 9
Richmond RD			
- Mortlake SD	1605*	ESR 10	Mfc Shelf 9
- Richmond SD	1605*		SC/C 9 & Mfc
Rotherhithe RD	1583*		
Southwark St George RD	1563-1565*		
Southwark St Olaf RD			
- St John Horsleydown SD	1559*	WSR 11	SC/C 9 & Mfc
- St Olaf & St Thomas SDs	1559*	WSR 10	SC/C 9 & Mfc
Southwark St Saviour RD			
- Christchurch & St Saviour SDs	1557-1558*	WSR 13	Mfc Shelf 9
Wandsworth RD	1576-1579	ESR 6 pts 1-4	Mfc Shelf 9
Windsor RD - Surrey part	1695	WSR 1	Mfc Shelf 9

SURREY **1861**   *= Microfilm held

REGISTRATION DISTRICT	RG 9	REGISTRATION DISTRICT	RG 9
Bermondsey RD	0319-0326	Farnham RD	0430-0433*
Bermondsey RD *part*	0322-0326*	Godstone RD	0445-0446*
Camberwell RD	0377-0388	Guildford RD	0424-0429*
Chertsey RD	0421-0423*	Hambledon RD	0437-0438*
Croydon RD	0447-0453	Kingston RD	0454-0458*
Dorking RD	0439-0441	Lambeth RD	0346-0367
Epsom RD	0418-0420	Newington RD	0335-0345*
Epsom RD *part*	0419-0420*	Reigate RD	0442-0444
Farnborough RD	0434-0436*	Richmond RD	0459-0461

60

REGISTRATION DISTRICT	RG 9	REGISTRATION DISTRICT	RG 9
Rotherhithe RD	0389-0391	Southwark St Saviour RD	0312-0315
Southwark St George RD	0327-0334	Wandsworth RD	0368-0376
Southwark St Olaf RD	0316-0318	Windsor RD	0368-0376

West Surrey FHS 1861 census indexes [WSR]

REGISTRATION DISTRICT	RG 9	Volume	Location
Guildford RD	0428 (ff5-144)	WSR 16	Mfc Shelf 9
Southwark RD			
- Christchurch, St Saviour & St Thomas SDs	0312-0316	WSR 14	Mfc Shelf 9

SURREY **1871**
Clive Ayton 1871 Census Index [CA]

REGISTRATION DISTRICT	RG 10		Location
St Olaf RD			
- St James Bermondsey SD	0633-0634	CA	SR/C 10 & Mfc
Wandsworth RD - Wandsworth SD	0704	CA	Mfc Shelf 9
Horley parish			SR/C 7 & SR/C 10

SURREY **1881**
GSU Transcript & Indexes - county complete [Lower Library Mfc]

SURREY **1891**
East Surrey FHS 1891 Census Index [ESR] & West Surrey FHS Records Series [WSR]

REGISTRATION DISTRICT	RG 12	Volume	Location
Lambeth RD			
- Waterloo Road SD	0387-0390	ESR 1 pt 1	Mfc Shelf 9
- Norwood SD	0412-0419	ESR 1 pt 2	Mfc Shelf 9
Worplesdon parish		WSR 18	SR/PER
Wyke parish		WSR 18	SR/PER

SUSSEX (SX)

1767 SX papist return (CRS Occ Paper 2) [RC/PER]
1801 Ticehurst [SX/C 10]
1821 Chiddingly [SX/C1&10]
Hartfield [SX/C 10]
Hastings St Mary in the Castle [SX/C 10]
1831 East Dean [SX/C 10]
Hastings St Clements [SX/C 10]
Hastings St Mary in the Castle [SX/C 10]
Lewes St John Sub Castro [SX/C 10]
Ticehurst [SX/C 10]
Uckfield [SX/C 10]
1838 Withyham inhabitants [Apply to Staff (Shelf 9)]

SUSSEX **1841**
Ashurst [Mfc Shelf 9]
Bodiam [SP 71/29 & SX/C 5]
Coombes [Mfc Shelf 9]
Felpham [SX/C 1]

Ferring [SX/C 1]
Folkington [SX/R 154]
Lodsworth [SX/C 16]

The 1841 districts were based upon the Hundreds.
The Society has films for the following Hundreds:

DISTRICT/HUNDRED	HO 107
Arundel/Avisford & Bury	1089-1091
West Easwrith	1092
Poling	1093
Rotherbridge	1094
Brightford/Burbeach	1095
East Easwrith/Fishergate/Patching & West Grinstead	1096
Singlecross	1097
Steyning/Taring/Tiphook/Windham & Ewhurst	1098
Aldwick/Bosham	1099
Box & Stockbridge/Dumpford & Easebourne	1100-1102
Manhood/Westbourne & Singleton/Baldstow/Battle/ Bexhill & Foxearle	1103-1105
Goldspur/Gostrow/Guestling & Hastings	1106-1107

SUSSEX **1851**
East Sussex - June Barnes [ESX];
Sussex FHG West Sussex 1851 Census Index [WSX]   * = Microfilm held

REGISTRATION DISTRICT	HO 107	Volume	Location
Battle RD	1636*	ESX 6-7	SX/C 4-5
Brighton RD	1644 -1646*		
Chichester RD	1653*		
Cuckfield RD	1642*	ESX 19-20	SX/C 9
Eastbourne RD	1637*	ESX 8	SX/C 5
East Grinstead RD	1641*	ESX 17-18	SX/C 7
Hailsham RD	1638*	ESX 9-10	SX/C 5
Hastings RD	1635*	ESX 4-5	SX/C 4
Horsham RD	1648*		
Lewes RD	1643*	ESX 21-23	SX/C 9
Midhurst RD	1654*	WSX 3-4	Shelf 9
Petworth RD	1649*		
Rye RD	1634*	ESX 2-3	SX/C 4
Steyning RD	1647*		
Thakenham RD	1650*	WSX 1-2	Shelf 9
Ticehurst RD	1639*	ESX 11-13	SX/C 5 & 7
Uckfield RD	1640*	ESX/14-16	SX/C 7
Westbourne RD	1655*		
Westhampnett RD	1652*		
Worthing RD	1651*		

East Sussex Workhouses 1851 Census Indexes:
Battle; Brighton; Chailey; Eastbourne; Newhaven; West Firle; East Grinstead; Cuckfield; Hailsham Union (Hellingley); Lewes; Hastings Union (Ore); Rye; Steyning Union (New Shoreham); Tichurst; Uckfield [Shelf 9]

SUSSEX **1861**   * = Microfilm held

REGISTRATION DISTRICT	RG 9
Battle RD	0563-0565*
Brighton RD	
- Kemptown SD *part*	0592*
- St Peter SD	0593-0598*

- Palace SD part 0599-0600*
Hastings RD
  - St Mary in Castle SD 0561*
  - All Saints SD 0562*
Horsham RD 0607-0609 (f 96)*
  - South Horsham SD 0607*
  - North Horsham SD 0608-0609*
Lewes RD 0584-0590*
Westbourne RD - Westbourne SD 0630*
Worthing RD 0614*-0616*

SUSSEX **1861-1891 inclusive**
Appledram [SX/C 12 & 13]   Itchenor, West [SX/C 12]
Ashurst [Mfc Shelf 9]   Lodsworth 1861-1871 [SX/C 14]
Birdham [SX/C 12 & 13]   Middleton [SX/C 1]
Coombes [Mfc Shelf 9]   Mundham, North [SX/C 12 & 13]
Donnington [SC/C 12 & 13]   Selsey [SX/C 1, 12 & 13]
Ernley [SX/C 12 & 13]   Siddlesham [SX/C 12 & 15]
Felpham [SX/C1]   Wittering, East [SX/C 12 & 13]
Ferring [SC/C 1]   Wittering, West [SX/C 12 & 13]
Hunston [SX/C 12 & 13]

SUSSEX **1881**
GSU Transcript & Indexes - county complete [Lower Library Mfc]

WARWICKSHIRE (WA)

1767 WA papist return (CRS Occ Paper 2) [RC/PER]
Birmingham: St Martin's papist return (Recusant Hist 15/5) [RC/PER]

1821 Southam [SP 72/28]
Bedworth [WA/C 17]

WARWICKSHIRE **1841**
Birmingham Districts 1& 2 [SP 72/9]
Coventry street index [WA/TR 2]

The 1841 districts were based upon the Hundreds.
The Society holds films for the following Hundreds:
DISTRICT/HUNDRED   **HO 107**
Kington   1131-1134
Knightlow - Kenilworth division   1135

WARWICKSHIRE **1851**
GSU 1851 Census Pilot Project Transcript & Indexes - county complete [Mfc]
Birmingham & Midland GS 1851 Census Index of Warwickshire [WAB]; Rugby FHG 1851
Census Index [RFG]; Oxfordshire FHS 1851 Transcripts & Index [OXF] & GSU 1851
Census Pilot Project **Warwickshire** including cross county districts [GSW]* = Microfilm held
REGISTRATION DISTRICT   **HO 107**   **Volume**   **Location**
Alcester RD   2075*   WAB 12   WA/C 1
Aston RD
  - Deritend/Duddleton SDs   2060-2061*   WAB   Mfc
  - Erdington & Sutton Coldfield SDs   2062*   WAB   Mfc

63

REGISTRATION DISTRICT	HO 107	Volume	Location
Atherstone RD	2064*		
Birmingham RD			
- Ladywood SD	2051*	WAB	Mfc
- St Thomas SD	2052*		Mfc
- St Martin SD	2053*		WA/C 1
- St Peter SD	2054*		Mfc
- St Philip's SD	2055*		Mfc
- St Paul SD	2056*		Mfc
- St Mary SD	2057*		
- St George SD	2058*		
- All Saints SD	2059*		
Birmingham street index			WA/C 16
Coventry RD	2067-2068*		
Coventry City street index			WA/TR2
Foleshill RD	2066*		
Meriden RD	2063		
Nuneaton RD	2065*		
Rugby RD	2069-2070*		
- St Matthew & St Andrew SDs (ff178-385)	2069*	RFG 1	Shelf 9
- Bilton, Brandon & Bretford, Brinklow, Brownsover, Church Lawford, Coombe Fields, Easenhall, Harborough Magna, Little Lawford, Long Lawford, Newbold, Newnham Regis, Wolston	2069*	RFG 2	Shelf 9
- whole RD except Rugby & Bilton SDs	2069-2070*	RFG	Mfc
Shipston on Stour RD	2076*	WAB 13	WA/C 1
Solihull RD	2071*	WAB 9	WA/C 1
Southam RD	2077*	WAB 14	WA/C 1
Stratford on Avon RD	2074*	WAB 11	WA/C 1
Banbury RD - Warwickshire part	1733-1734*	OXF 9	OX/C 10-11
Chipping Norton RD - Warwickshire part	1732	GSW	Mfc
Kings Norton RD - Edgbaston SD	2049*	WAB	Mfc
Tamworth RD - Warwickshire part	2013*	GSW	Mfc

Warwickshire 1851 Census Transcripts & Index - Relative Reflections [WAR]. Please note exact Piece Numbers or Districts are not given in the earlier volumes. Thus the contents are listed by parish.

PARISH	Volume	Location	PARISH	Volume	Location
Allesley	WAR 11	WA/C 6	Balsall	WAR 1	WA/C 2
Ansley	WAR 9	WA/C 5	Barcheston	WAR 3	WA/C 2
Ansty	WAR 1	WA/C 2	Barston	WAR 1	WA/C 2
Arley	WAR 6	WA/C 3	Baxterley	WAR 12	WA/C 7
Arrow	WAR 15	WA/C 8	Bearley	WAR 14	WA/C 8
Ashow	WAR 3	WA/C 2	Beaudesert	WAR 2	WA/C 2
Astley	WAR 6	WA/C 3	Beausale	WAR 16	WA/C 9
Atherstone on Stour	WAR 8	WA/C 4	Bentley nr Shustoke	WAR 15	WA/C 8
Austrey	WAR 17	WA/C 9	Berkswell	WAR 19	WA/C 10
Baddesley Clinton	WAR 1	WA/C 2	Bickenhill	WAR 10	WA/C 5
Baddesley Ensor	WAR 17	WA/C 9	Billesley	WAR 6	WA/C 3
Bagington	WAR 9	WA/C 5	Binley	WAR 1	WA/C 2

PARISH	Volume	Location	PARISH	Volume	Location
Binton	WAR 6	WA/C 3	Lighthorne	WAR 5	WA/C 3
Birdingbury	WAR 6	WA/C 3	Lillington	WAR 2	WA/C 2
Bishops Itchington	WAR 14	WA/C 8	Loxley	WAR 12	WA/C 7
Bourton on Dunsmore	WAR 11	WA/C 6	Marton	WAR 8	WA/C 4
Brailes	WAR 18	WA/C 10	Maxstoke	WAR 2	WA/C 2
Brownsover	WAR 7	WA/C 4	Merevale	WAR 15	WA/C 8
Bubbenhall	WAR 4	WA/C 3	Meriden	WAR 19	WA/C 10
Burmington	WAR 5	WA/C 3	Minworth	WAR 12	WA/C 7
Burton Dassett	WAR 18	WA/C 10	Moreton Bagot	WAR 11	WA/C 6
Butlers Marston	WAR 4	WA/C 3	Moreton Morrell	WAR 7	WA/C 4
Caldecote	WAR 4	WA/C 3	Newbold on Avon	WAR 5	WA/C 3
Chadshunt	WAR 5	WA/C 3	Newbold Pacy	WAR 15	WA/C 8
Charlecote	WAR 6	WA/C 3	Newnham Regis	WAR 2	WA/C 2
Cherington	WAR 18	WA/C 10	Newton and Biggin	WAR 15	WA/C 8
Chesterton	WAR 14	WA/C 8	Newton Regis	WAR 17	WA/C 9
Church Lawford	WAR 12	WA/C 7	No Mans Heath ep	WAR 17	WA/C 9
Churchover	WAR 15	WA/C 8	Norton Lindsay	WAR 8	WA/C 4
Claverdon	WAR 5	WA/C 3	Nuthurst	WAR 1	WA/C 2
Clifton on Dunsmore	WAR 15	WA/C 8	Oversley	WAR 15	WA/C 8
Coleshill	WAR 7	WA/C 4	Oxhilll	WAR 10	WA/C 5
Compton Verney	WAR 6	WA/C 3	Packington, Great	WAR 1	WA/C 2
Compton Wyniates	WAR 3	WA/C 2	Packington, Little	WAR 1	WA/C 2
Coombe Fields	WAR 12	WA/C 7	Packwood	WAR 2	WA/C 2
Corley	WAR 10	WA/C 5	Pillerton Hersey	WAR 4	WA/C 3
Coughton	WAR 13	WA/C 7	Pillerton Priors	WAR 7	WA/C 4
Counden nr Coventry	WAR 10	WA/C 5	Polesworth	WAR 17	WA/C 9
Curdworth	WAR 12	WA/C 7	Preston Bagot	WAR 4	WA/C 3
Dunchurch	WAR 16	WA/C 9	Priors Hardwick	WAR 9	WA/C 5
Elmdon	WAR 1	WA/C 2	Priors Marston	WAR 19	WA/C 10
Exhall nr Alcester	WAR 3	WA/C 2	Radbourn, Lower	WAR 5	WA/C 3
Fenny Compton	WAR 18	WA/C 10	Radbourn, Upper	WAR 5	WA/C 3
Fillongley	WAR 19	WA/C 10	Salford Priors	WAR 6	WA/C 3
Gaydon	WAR 5	WA/C 3	Sambourn	WAR 13	WA/C 7
Grandborough	WAR 6	WA/C 3	Seckington	WAR 17	WA/C 9
Grendon	WAR 17	WA/C 9	Sheldon	WAR 10	WA/C 5
Halford	WAR 10	WA/C 5	Sherbourne	WAR 12	WA/C 7
Hampton in Arden	WAR 19	WA/C 10	Shilton	WAR 1	WA/C 2
Hampton Lucy	WAR 9	WA/C 5	Shrewley	WAR 16	WA/C 9
Harborough Magna	WAR 12	WA/C 7	Shuckburgh, Lower	WAR 10	WA/C 5
Haseley	WAR 16	WA/C 9	Shuckburgh, Upper	WAR 10	WA/C 5
Haselor	WAR 13	WA/C 7	Shustoke	WAR 2	WA/C 2
Hatton	WAR 16	WA/C 9	Shuttington	WAR 17	WA/C 9
Hodnell	WAR 5	WA/C 3	Solihull	WAR 4	WA/C 3
Honiley	WAR 16	WA/C 9	Spernall	WAR 11	WA/C 6
Honington	WAR 11	WA/C 6	Stivichall	WAR 9	WA/C 5
Idlicote	WAR 3	WA/C 2	Stoneleigh	WAR 16	WA/C 9
Ilmington	WAR 18	WA/C 10	Stourton	WAR 13	WA/C 7
Kinwalsey	WAR 19	WA/C 10	Stratford on Avon	WAR 8	WA/C 4
Kinwarton	WAR 13	WA/C 7	Stretton on Fosse	WAR 13	WA/C 7
Knowle	WAR 1	WA/C 2	Sutton under Brailes	WAR 4	WA/C 3
Ladbroke	WAR 5	WA/C 3	Tamworth in Arden	WAR 9	WA/C 5
Langley	WAR 14	WA/C 8	Thurlaston	WAR 16	WA/C 9
Lapworth	WAR 3	WA/C 2	Tysoe	WAR 13	WA/C 7
Lawford, Little	WAR 5	WA/C 3	Ufton	WAR 7	WA/C 4
Lea Marston	WAR 1	WA/C 2	Wappenbury	WAR 2	WA/C 2

PARISH	Volume	Location	PARISH	Volume	Location
Warwick St Mary pt	WAR 11	WA/C 6	Whiteacre, Over	WAR 2	WA/C 2
Warwick St Mary pt	WAR 14	WA/C 8	Willoughby	WAR 9	WA/C 5
Wasperton	WAR 2	WA/C 2	Wishaw	WAR 5	WA/C 3
Watergall	WAR 5	WA/C 3	Withybroook	WAR 1	WA/C 2
Weddington	WAR 4	WA/C 3	Wixford	WAR 3	WA/C 2
Weethley	WAR 6	WA/C 3	Wolford, Great	WAR 8	WA/C 4
Weston Under			Wolford, Little	WAR 8	WA/C 4
Wetherley	WAR 2	WA/C 2	Wolverton	WAR 14	WA/C 8
Whatcott	WAR 7	WA/C 4	Wormleighton	WAR 7	WA/C 4
Whichford with Ascott	WAR 13	WA/C 7	Wroxhall	WAR 2	WA/C 2
Whitchurch	WAR 8	WA/C 4	Wyken	WAR 1	WA/C 2
Whiteacre, Nether	WAR 9	WA/C 5			

WARWICKSHIRE 1861   * = Microfilm held

REGISTRATION DISTRICT	RG 9	REGISTRATION DISTRICT	RG 9
Alcester RD	2233-2236*	**Birmingham RD** (*continued*)	
Aston RD		- St Mary SD	2153-2155*
- Deritend SD *part*	2169-2174*	- St George SD	2156-2164*
- Duddeston SD	2175-2181*	**Nuneaton RD**	
- Erdington SD	2182-2186*	- Nuneaton SD *part*	2194*
Atherstone RD	2191-2193*	**Rugby RD**	2210-2214*
Birmingham RD		**Shipston on Stour RD**	2237-2240*
- Ladywood SD *part*	2129-2133*	**Solihull RD**	2215-2218*
- St Thomas SD	2134-2139*	**Southam RD**	2241-2243*
- St Martin SD	2140-2145*	**Stratford on Avon RD**	
- St Peter SD	2146-2148*	- Stratford SD *part*	2230*
- St Philip SD	2149-2150*	- Old Stratford SD	2231*
- St Paul SD	2151-2152*	- Wootton Wawen SD	2232*

Birmingham street index [WA/C 16]

WARWICKSHIRE 1881
GSU Transcripts & Indexes - county complete [Lower Library Mfc]

WESTMORLAND (WE)

1767 WE papist return (*in 2 vols*) (CRS Occ Papers 1 & 2) [RC/PER]
1787 WE census [WE/C 3]

WESTMORLAND **1841**
The 1841 districts were based upon the Hundreds.
The Society holds films for the following Hundreds:
DISTRICT/HUNDRED   HO 107
Kendal or Kirby Kendal *part*   1160

WESTMORLAND **1851**   No microfilms held
Cumbria FHS 1851 Census Indexes [CUF];
North Westmorland 1851 Census Index [NWE]
REGISTRATION DISTRICT   HO 107   Volume   Location
East Ward RD
  - Orton SD   2439 ff418-532   CUF & NWE   WE/C 5 & 1

Kendal RD
- Ambleside, Grayrigg &
  Kirkby Lonsdale *part* SDs   2441 ff1-682   CUF   WE/C 2
- Kendal *part* & Milnthorp SDs   2442 ff1-110,   CUF   WE/C 4
                                    205-303,400-684
West Ward RD
- Morland & Lowther SDs   2440 ff1-329 end CUF & NWE WE/C 4 &

WESTMORLAND **1851** 2% Sample [Surname Index] [Mfc]
Fawcet Forest; Winton

WESTMORLAND **1861**   * = Microfilm held
REGISTRATION DISTRICT   RG 9
East Ward RD   3956-3960*
Kendal RD   3963-3973
West Ward RD   3961-3962

WESTMORLAND **1881**
GSU Transcript & Indexes - county complete [Mfc]

WILTSHIRE (WL)

1697 Clyffe Pypard [WL/C 16]; Hilmarton [WL/C 16]; Tockenham [WL/C 16]
1767 WL papist return (CRS Occ Paper 2) [RC/PER]
1787 Chisleden census (WL FHS J 35-36) [WL/PER]
1801 Horningsham [WL/C 16]
      Woodborough (WL FHS J 62) [WL/PER]
1811 Woodborough cen (WL FHS J 34) [WL/PER]

WILTSHIRE **1841**
The Society has films for the following Hundreds:
DISTRICT/HUNDRED   HO 107
Cawden/Cadworth/Chalk   1169-1170
Chippenham   1171-1172
North Damerham   1173

WILTSHIRE **1841-1891**
Highworth Union workhouse at Stratton St Mary [WL/C 16]

WILTSHIRE **1851**   * = Microfilm held
REGISTRATION DISTRICT   HO 107   REGISTRATION DISTRICT   HO 107
Alderbury RD   1846   Pewsey RD   1844
Amesbury RD   1845   Salisbury RD   1847
Bradford on Avon RD   1841   Tisbury RD   1849
Calne RD   1837   Warminster RD   1843
Chippenham RD   1836   Westbury RD   1842
Cricklade RD   1834   Wilton RD   1848
Devizes RD   1839   Andover RD - Wiltshire part   1683*
Highworth RD   1833   Cirencester RD - Wiltshire part 1968*
Malmesbury RD   1835   Hungerford RD - Wiltshire part 1686*
Marlborough RD   1838   New Forest RD - Wiltshire part 1668*
Melksham RD   1840   Romsey RD - Wiltshire part   1671*
Mere RD   1850

WILTSHIRE **1851**
Wiltshire 1851 Census Indexes - Barbara Carter et al. for the NIMROD Index.
Organised parish by parish NOT by Piece Number or District. Shelved at WL/C 1-10

PARISH	Location	PARISH	Location
Aldbourne	WL/C 1	Bromham	WL/C 9
Alderbury	WL/C 8	Broughton Gifford	WL/C 9
Alderton	WL/C 1	Bulkington	WL/C 1
All Cannings	WL/C 1	Bullbridge	WL/C 3
Allington	WL/C 8	Burbage	WL/C 1
Alton Barnes	WL/C 1	Burcombe	WL/C 1
Alton Priors	WL/C 1	Buttermere	WL/C 1
Alvediston	WL/C 1	Calne	WL/C 9
Amesbury	WL/C 8	Calstone Wellington	WL/C 10
Ansty	WL/C 1	Castle Combe	WL/C 2
Ashton Keynes	WL/C 8	Castle Eaton	WL/C 2
Ashton, West	WL/C 1	Chalfield	WL/C 9
Atworth	WL/C 8	Charlton (nr Malmesbury)	WL/C 9
Avebury	WL/C 8	Charlton Pewsey	WL/C 2
Badbury	WL/C 1	Chernhill	WL/C 9
Barford St Martin	WL/C 8	Cheverel, Great	WL/C 2
Baverstock	WL/C 9	Cheverel, Little	WL/C 2
Bayden	WL/C 1	Chicklade	WL/C 9
Bedwyn, Great	WL/C 1	Chilmark	WL/C 9
Bedwyn, Little	WL/C 8	Chilton Foliot	WL/C 9
Beechingstoke	WL/C 1	Chippenham	WL/C 2
Bemerton	WL/C 8	Chirton	WL/C 9
Berwick Bassett	WL/C 8	Chisleden	WL/C 2
Berwick St James	WL/C 8	Chitterne All Saints	WL/C 2
Berwick St John	WL/C 1	Chitterne St Mary	WL/C 2
Berwick St Leonard	WL/C 8	Chittoe	WL/C 9
Biddestone St Leonards	WL/C 1	Cholderton	WL/C 8
Biddestone St Peter	WL/C 1	Christian Malford	WL/C 9
Bishops Cannings	WL/C 1	Chute	WL/C 2
Bishopstone	WL/C 1	Chute Forest	WL/C 2
Bishopstone (South Wiltshire)	WL/C 8	Clarendon Park	WL/C 9
Bishopstrow	WL/C 8	Clyffe Pypard	WL/C 2
Blackland	WL/C 8	Codford St Mary	WL/C 9
Blunsden St Andrew	WL/C 1	Codford St Peter	WL/C 9
Bodenham	WL/C 12	Colerne	WL/C 2
Boscombe	WL/C 8	Colingbourne Ducis	WL/C 2
Bower Chalk	WL/C 8	Collingbourne Kingston	WL/C 9
Box	WL/C 1	Compton Basssett	WL/C 9
Boyton	WL/C 8	Compton Chamberlain	WL/C 9
Bradford on Avon	WL/C 8	Coombe Bissett	WL/C 9
Bradley, North	WL/C 8	Corsham	WL/C 2
Bratton	WL/C 8	Corsley	WL/C 2
Bremhill	WL/C 8	Corsley (parts 3 & 4)	WL/C 9
Bremilham	WL/C 8	Coulston, East	WL/C 2
Brinkworth	WL/C 8	Cricklade St Mary	WL/C 2
Britford	WL/C 9	Cricklade St Sampson	WL/C 2
Brixton Deverill	WL/C 1	Crudwell	WL/C 9
Broad Blunsden	WL/C 9	Dauntsey	WL/C 10
Broad Chalke	WL/C 9	Derry Hill	WL/C 10
Broad Hinton	WL/C 9	Devizes St John	WL/C 3
Brokenborough	WL/C 9	Devizes St Mary	WL/C 3

PARISH	Location	PARISH	Location
Devizes Workhouse	WL/C 3	Hindon	WL/C 11
Dilton Marsh	WL/C 10	Hinton in Steeple Ashton	WL/C 11
Dinton	WL/C 10	Hinton, Little	WL/C 11
Ditchampton	WL/C 3	Hippenscombe	WL/C 13
Ditteridge	WL/C 3	Holt	WL/C 11
Donhead St Andrew	WL/C 3	Homington	WL/C 11
Donhead St Mary	WL/C 3	Horningsham	WL/C 4
Downton	WL/C 10	Huish	WL/C 4
Drayton Cerne	WL/C 10	Hullavington	WL/C 11
Durnnford	WL/C 10	Hungerford - Workhouse	WL/C 11
Durrington	WL/C 10	Idmiston	WL/C 11
Easterton	WL/C 10	Iford	WL/C 14
Easton Grey	WL/C 10	Imber	WL/C 4
Easton, Royal	WL/C 10	Inglesham	WL/C 4
Ebbesbourne Wake	WL/C 10	Keevil	WL/C 11
Edington	WL/C 10	Kennet, East	WL/C 11
Eisey	WL/C 3	Kilmington	WL/C 11
Enford	WL/C 3	Kingston Deverill	WL/C 4
Erlestoke	WL/C 3	Kington Langley	WL/C 11
Etchilhampton	WL/C 3	Kington St Michael	WL/C 4
Everleigh	WL/C 10	Kington, West	WL/C 4
Farley	WL/C 12	Knock	WL/C 11
Fiddington	WL/C 10	Knoyle, East	WL/C 4
Fifield (near Overton)	WL/C 10	Knoyle, West	WL/C 12
Fifield Bavant	WL/C 10	Lacock	WL/C 11
Figheldean	WL/C 10	Lanfdord	WL/C 12
Fisherton Anger -		Langford, Little	WL/C 4
Gaol, Asylum & Hospital	WL/C 3	Langley Burrrell	WL/C 4
Fittleton	WL/C 10	Latton	WL/C 11
Fonthill Bishop	WL/C 10	Laverstock	WL/C 4
Fonthill Gifford	WL/C 10	Lavington, West	WL/C 4
Fosbury	WL/C 13	Lea	WL/C 11
Fovant	WL/C 10	Leigh Delamere	WL/C 4
Foxley	WL/C 8	Leigh, The	WL/C 4
Freshford	WL/C 10	Liddington	WL/C 4
Froxfield	WL/C 10	Limpley Stoke	WL/C 11
Fyfield	WL/C 3	Littleton Drew	WL/C 4
Garsdon	WL/C 10	Littleton Pannell	WL/C 11
Grimstead, East	WL/C 3	Longbridge Deverill	WL/C 11
Grimstead, West	WL/C 3	Luckington	WL/C 11
Grittenham	WL/C 10	Ludgershall	WL/C 4
Grittleton	WL/C 3	Lydiard Millicent	WL/C 4
Ham	WL/C 3	Lydiard Tregoze	WL/C 4
Hankerton	WL/C 10	Lyneham	WL/C 11
Hannnington	WL/C 3	Maddington	WL/C 11
Hardenhuish	WL/C 3	Maiden Bradley	WL/C 11
Harnham, East	WL/C 10	Malmesbury	WL/C 11
Harnham, West	WL/C 3	Manningford Abbots	WL/C 4
Heddington	WL/C 10	Manningford Bohune	WL/C 4
Heytesbury	WL/C 10	Manningford Bruce	WL/C 4
Highway	WL/C 10	Marden	WL/C 4
Highworth	WL/C 4	Market Lavington	WL/C 4
Hill Deverill	WL/C 4	Marlborough College	WL/C 11
Hilmarton	WL/C 10	Marlborough St Mary	WL/C 11
Hilperton	WL/C 10	Marlborough St Peter	WL/C 11

PARISH	Location	PARISH	Location
Marston Meysey	WL/C 4	Shalbourne	WL/C 13
Marston, South	WL/C 4	Sherrington	WL/C 13
Melchet	WL/C 12	Sherston Magna	WL/C 13
Melksham	WL/C 12	Sherston Parva	WL/C 13
Mere	WL/C 12	Shrewton	WL/C 6
Mildenhall	WL/C 12	Slaughterford	WL/C 6
Milford	WL/C 12	Somerford, Great	WL/C 13
Milston	WL/C 5	Somerford, Little	WL/C 13
Milton Lilbourne	WL/C 5	Sopworth	WL/C 13
Minety	WL/C 12	Southbroom St James (Devizes)	WL/C 6
Monkton Deverill	WL/C 12	Stanton Fitzwaren	WL/C 6
Monkton Farleigh	WL/C 12	Stanton St Bernard	WL/C 6
Netheravon	WL/C 5	Stanton St Quintln	WL/C 6
Nettleton	WL/C 5	Stapleford	WL/C 13
Newnton, North	WL/C 5	Staverton	WL/C 13
Newton Tony	WL/C 12	Steeple Ashton	WL/C 6
Newton, South	WL/C 12	Steeple Langford	WL/C 13
Norton	WL/C 8	Stert	WL/C 6
Norton Bavant	WL/C 5	Stockton	WL/C 13
Nunton	WL/C 12	Stourton	WL/C 13
Oaksey	WL/C 12	Stratford sub Castle	WL/C 13
Odstock	WL/C 12	Stratford Tony	WL/C 11
Ogbourne St Andrew	WL/C 12	Stratton St Margaret	WL/C 6
Ogbourne St George	WL/C 12	- ditto - Workhouse	WL/C 6
Orcheston St George	WL/C 5	Sutton Benger	WL/C 13
Orcheston St Mary	WL/C 5	Sutton Mandeville	WL/C 6
Overton	WL/C 12	Sutton Veny	WL/C 6
Patney	WL/C 5	Swallowcliffe	WL/C 13
Pewsey	WL/C 5	Swindon	WL/C 6
Pewsey - Workhouse	WL/C 5	Swindon (parts 5-6)	WL/C 13
Pewsham	WL/C 12	Teffont Evias	WL/C 13
Pitton	WL/C 12	Teffont Magna	WL/C 13
Porton	WL/C 11	Tidcombe	WL/C 13
Potterne	WL/C 5	Tidworth, North	WL/C 6
Poulshot	WL/C 5	Tidworth, South	WL/C 13
Preshute	WL/C 12	Tilshead	WL/C 6
Purton	WL/C 12	Tisbury, East	WL/C 6
Quidhampton	WL/C 8	Tisbury, West	WL/C 6
Radbury	WL/C 1	Tockenham	WL/C 6
Ramsbury	WL/C 5	Tollard Royal	WL/C 6
Rodbourne Cheyney	WL/C 5	Trowbridge	WL/C 6
Rollestone	WL/C 5	Trowbridge (parts 5-10)	WL/C 13
Rowde	WL/C 5	Tytherton Kelloways	WL/C 13
Rushall	WL/C 5	Upavon	WL/C 7
Salisbury Cathedrral	WL/C 5	Upton Lovell	WL/C 14
Salisbury St Edmund	WL/C 12	Upton Scudamore	WL/C 7
Salisbury St Martin	WL/C 5	Urchfont	WL/C 7
Salisbury St Martin (pts 3-5)	WL/C 13	Wanborough	WL/C 7
Salisbury St Thomas	WL/C 5	Wardour	WL/C 14
Seagry	WL/C 6	Warminster	WL/C 7
Sedgehill	WL/C 13	Westbury	WL/C 14
Seend	WL/C 13	Westport St Mary	WL/C 14
Semington	WL/C 13	Westwood	WL/C 14
Semley	WL/C 13	Westwood - Workhouse	WL/C 14
Sevenhampton	WL/C 6	Whiteparish	WL/C 14

PARISH	Location	PARISH	Location
Wilcot	WL/C 7	Wishford, Great	WL/C 14
Wilsford (near Pewsey)	WL/C 14	Woodborough	WL/C 14
Wilsford cum Lake		Woodford	WL/C 14
(near Amesbury)	WL/C 14	Wooton Bassett	WL/C 7
Wilton	WL/C 7	Wooton Rivers	WL/C 14
Winsley	WL/C 14	Wraxall, South	WL/C 14
Winterbourne Bassett	WL/C 14	Wraxhall, North	WL/C 7
Winterbourne Dauntsey	WL/C 14	Wroughton	WL/C 14
Winterbourne Earls	WL/C 14	Wylye	WL/C 7
Winterbourne Gunner	WL/C 14	Yatesbury	WL/C 14
Winterbourne Monkton	WL/C 14	Yatton Keynell	WL/C 7
Winterbourne Stoke	WL/C 14	Zeals	WL/C 7
Winterslow	WL/C 14		

WILTSHIRE **1851-1891**
Imber [WL/C 16]

WILTSHIRE **1861**   * = Microfilm held

REGISTRATION DISTRICT	RG 9	REGISTRATION DISTRICT	RG 9
Alderbury RD	1313-1315*	**Marlborough RD**	1288-1289
Amesbury RD	1310-1312*	**Melksham RD**	1294-1296
Bradford on Avon RD	1297-1299	**Mere RD**	1323-1324*
Calne RD	1286-1287	**Pewsey RD**	1307-1309*
Chippenham RD	1280-1285	**Salisbury RD**	1316-1317*
Cricklade RD	1273-1275*	**Tisbury RD**	1320-1322*
Devizes RD	1290-1293	**Warminster RD**	1303-1306*
Highworth RD	1268-1272*	**Westbury RD**	1300-1302
Malmesbury RD	1276-1279	**Wilton RD**	1318-1319*
- Malmesbury SD East	1276*		

WILTSHIRE **1871**
Wiltshire 1871 Census Index - Mary Kearns Trace [WLT]
WLT 1-8 shelved at WL/C 18, WLT 9-14 Mfc

PARISH	Volume	PARISH	Volume
Albourne	WLT 4	Beechingstoke	WLT 2
Alderbury	WLT 9	Berwick Bassett	WLT 4
All Cannings	WLT 1	Bishops Canning	WLT 1
Allington	WLT 1	Bishopstone (North Wilts)	WLT 7
Allington	WLT 10	Bishipstone (South Wilts)	WLT 13
Alton Barnes	WLT 1	Blackland	WLT 4
Alton Priors	WLT 2	Bodenham	WLT 9
Alvediston	WLT 14	Boscombe	WLT 10
Amesbury	WLT 10	Bower Chalk	WLT 13
Anstey	WL:T 14	Bowood	WLT 6
Avebury	WLT 4	Boyton	WLT 13
Avon (Extra Parochial)	WLT 6	Bramshaw	WLT 9
Barford St Martin	WLT 13	Bremhill	WLT 6
Baverstock	WLT 13	Britford	WLT 9
Baydon	WLT 6	Brixton Deverill	WLT 14
Bedwyn, Great	WLT 11	Broad Chalk	WLT 13
Bedwyn, Little	WLT 11	Broad Hinton	WLT 4
Berwick St James	WLT 13	Bromham	WLT 1
Berwick St John	WLT 14	Bulford	WLT 10
Berwick St Leonard	WLT 14	Burbage	WLT 11

PARISH	Volume	PARISH	Volume
Burcombe	WLT 13	Fonthil Gifford	WLT 14
Buttermere	WLT 11	Fovant	WLT 13
Calne	WLT 6	Froxfield	WLT 11
Calstone Wellington	WLT 4	Fuggleston St Peter	WLT 13
Charlton	WLT 2	Fullaway	WLT 1
Cherhill	WLT 4	Fyfield	WLT 4
Cheverell, Great	WLT 2	Grimstead, East	WLT 9
Cheverell, Little	WLT 2	Grimstead, West	WLT 9
Chicklade	WLT 14	Groveley Wood e.p.	WLT 13
Chilmark	WLT 14	Ham	WLT 11
Chilton Foliat	WLT 11	Harnham, West	WLT 9
Chirton	WLT 2	Heytsbury	WLT 13
Chisledon	WLT 7	Highway	WLT 4
Chittoe	WLT 1	Hill Deverill	WLT 14
Chitterne All Saints	WLT 13	Hindon	WLT 14
Chitterne St Mary	WLT 13	Hinton Parva	WLT 7
Cholderton	WLT 10	Hippenscombe	WLT 11
Christian Malford	WLT 6	Horningsham	WLT 14
Chute	WLT 11	Hornington	WLT 9
Chute Forest	WLT 11	Huish	WLT 2
Clarendon Park	WLT 10	Hungerford (Wiltshire part)	WLT 11
Clatford Park	WLT 4	Hungerford Workhouse (Berks)	WLT 11
Clyffe Pypard	WLT 1	Idmiston	WLT 10
Codford St Mary	WLT 13	Imber	WLT 13
Codford St Peter	WLT 13	Kennett, East	WLT 4
Collingbourne Ducis	WLT 11	Kingston Deverill	WLT 14
Collingbourne Kingston	WLT 11	Kingston Langley	WLT 6
Compton Bassett	WLT 4	Kington St Michael	WLT 6
Coombe Bissett	WLT 9	Knook	WLT 13
Damerham	WLT 9	Knoyle, East	WLT 14
Dean, West	WLT 9	Knoyle, West	WLT 14
Devizes St John	WLT 3	Lake	WLT 10
Devizes St Mary	WLT 3	Landford	WLT 9
Donhead St Andrew	WLT 14	Langford, Little	WLT 13
Donhead St Mary	WLT 14	Langley Wood	WLT 9
Downton	WLT 9	Laverstock	WLT 10
Draycot Cerne	WLT 6	Liddington	WLT 7
Draycot Foliat	WLT 7	Longbridge, Deverill	WLT 14
Durnford	WLT 10	Ludgershall	WLT 11
Durrington	WLT 10	Lydiard Tregoze	WLT 7
Easton Royal	WLT 11	Lyneham	WLT 7
Ebbesbourne Wake	WLT 13	Maddington	WLT 13
Enford	WLT 11	Maiden Bradley	WLT 14
Erldoms	WLT 9	Manningford Abbots	WLT 2
Erlestoke	WLT 3	Manningford Bohune	WLT 2
Etchilhampton	WLT 1	Manningford Bruce	WLT 2
Everleigh	WLT 11	Marden	WLT 2
Farley	WLT 10	Market Lavington	WLT 2
Fifield Bavant	WLT 13	Marlborough College	WLT 5
Figheldean	WLT 10	Marlborough St Mary	WLT 5
Fisherton Anger	WLT 12	Marlborough SS Peter & Paul	WLT 5
Fisherton Delamere	WLT 13	Marston Tything (Potterne)	WLT 3
Fisherton House (Asylum)	WLT 10	Martin	WLT 9
Fittleton	WLT 11	Mere	WLT 14
Fonthill Bishop	WLT 14	Melchet Park	WLT 9

PARISH	Volume	PARISH	Volume
Mildenhall	WLT 5	Steeple Langford	WLT 13
Milford	WLT 10	Stockton	WLT 13
Milston	WLT 10	Stourton	WLT 14
Milton Lilbourne	WLT 11	Stratford Sub Castle	WLT 10
Monkton Deverill	WLT 14	Sutton Benger	WLT 6
Netheravon	WLT 11	Sutton Mandeville	WLT 14
Netherhampton	WLT 13	Sutton Veney	WLT 14
Newton Tony	WLT 10	Swallowcliffe	WLT 14
Newton, South	WLT 13	Swindon	WLT 8
No Mans Land	WLT 9	Teffont Evias	WLT 14
Nunton	WLT 9	Teffont Magna	WLT 14
Odstock	WLT 9	Tidcombe	WLT 11
Ogbourne St Andrew	WLT 4	Tidworth, North	WLT 11
Ogbourne St George	WLT 4	Tilshead	WLT 13
Orcheston St George	WLT 13	Tisbury	WLT 14
Orcheston St Mary	WLT 13	Tockenham	WLT 7
Overton Heath	WLT 4	Tollard Royal	WLT 14
Overton, West	WLT 4	Tytherton Kellaways	WLT 6
Perton Wood	WLT 14	Upavon	WLT 2
Pewsey	WLT 11	Upton Lovell	WLT 13
Pitton & Farley	WLT 10	Urchfont	WLT 2
Plaitford	WLT 9	Wanborough	WLT 7
Potterne	WLT 3	Wardour	WLt 14
Poulshot	WLT 3	Wellow, West	WLT 9
Preshute	WLT 4	Whiteparish	WLT 9
Ramsbury	WLT 5	Whitsbury	WLT 9
Rollestone	WLT 13	Wilcot	WLT 2
Rowde	WLT 1	Wilsford & Lake	WLT 10
Salsbury St Edmund	WLT 12	Wilsford (near Pewsey)	WLT 2
Salisbury St Martin	WLT 12	Wilton	WLT 13
Salisbury St Thomas	WLT 12	Winterbourne Bassett	WLT 4
Sarum, Old	WLT 10	Winterbourne Dauntsey	WLT 10
Savernake, North	WLT 5	Winterbourne Earls	WLT 10
Savernake, South	WLT 5	Winterbourne Gunner	WLT 10
Seagry	WLT 6	Winterbourne Monkton	WLT 4
Sedgehill	WLT 14	Winterbourne Stoke	WLT 13
Semley	WLT 14	Winterslow	WLT 10
Shalbourne	WLT 11	Wishford, Great	WLT 13
Sherrington	WLT 13	Woodborough	WLT 2
Shrewton	WLT 13	Woodford	WLT 10
Southbroom St James	WLT 1	Wooton Bassett	WLT 7
Standlinch	WLT 9	Wootton Rivers	WLT 11
Stanton St Bernard	WLT 1	Worton Tything (Potterne)	WLT 3
Stanton St Quinton	WLT 6	Wroughton	WLT 7
Stapleford	WLT 13	Wyle	WLT 13
		Yatesbury	WLT 4

WILTSHIRE **1881**
GSU Transcripts & Indexes - county complete [Lower Library Mfc]

WORCESTERSHIRE (WO)

1767 WO papist return (CRS Occ Paper 2) [RC/PER]

WORCESTERSHIRE 1841
The 1841 districts were based upon the Hundreds.
The Society holds films for the following Hundreds:
DISTRICT/HUNDRED	HO 107
Doddingtree *part* & Halfshire *part*	1194-1195
Oswaldstow	1201-1203
Pershore	1205-1206

WORCESTERSHIRE 1841-1881
Frankley [WO/L 44]

WORCESTERSHIRE 1851   * = Microfilm held
Birmingham & Midland GS 1851 Census Index of Worcestershire [WOB]

REGISTRATION DISTRICT	HO 107	Volume	Location
Bromsgrove RD	2047*	WOB 10	WO/C 10
Droitwich RD	2046*		
Evesham RD	2044*		
Kidderminster RD	2037-2038*	WOB 2	WO/C 2
Kings Norton RD			
- Kings Norton SD	2048*		
- Edgbaston SD	2049*		Mfc [WA]
- Harborne SD	2050*		Mfc [WA]
Martley RD	2041*		
Pershore RD	2045*		
Stourbridge RD			
- Halesowen SD	2034*		WO/C 1
- Stourbridge SD	2035*		WO/C 1A
- Kingswinford SD	2036*		ST/C 14
Tenbury RD	2040*		
Upton on Severn RD	2043*		
Worcester RD	2042*	WOB 6	WO/C 6
Alcester RD - Worcestershire part	2075*		
Cleobury Mortimer RD - Worcs. part	1985*		

WORCESTERSHIRE 1851 2% Sample [Surname Index] [Mfc]
Ashton Underhill; Pedmore; Sapey Lower; Stockton; Wadborough

WORCESTERSHIRE 1861   * = Microfilm held
REGISTRATION DISTRICT	RG 9	REGISTRATION DISTRICT	RG 9
Bromsgrove RD		- Harborne SD	2125-2127*
- Bromsgrove SD	2113-2115*	Martley RD	2085-2088*
Droitwich RD	2108-2112*	Pershore RD	2104-2107*
Evesham RD	2100-2103*	Stourbridge RD	2064-2074*
Kidderminster RD	2075-2082*	Tenbury RD	2083-2084*
Kings Norton RD		Upton on Severn RD	2096-2099*
- Kings Norton SD	2119-2121	Worcester RD	2089-2095*
- Kings Norton SD *part*	2120-2121*		
- Edgbaston SD	2122-2124*		

74

WORCESTERSHIRE 1881
GSU Transcript & Indexes - county complete [Lower Library Mfc]

YORKSHIRE - EAST RIDING (YKER)

1801-1821 York St. Giles [YK/C 54]
1811   York St. Maurice [YK/C 53]
1841-1871 Heslington St. Lawrence & St. Paul [YK/C 48]

YORKSHIRE - EAST RIDING 1841
The 1841 districts were based upon the Wapentakes.
The Society holds the following films.
DISTRICT/WAPENTAKE   HO 107
Buckrose & Dickering *parts* 1211-1214
Harthill   1218-1219
Holderness *part*   1223-1225

YORKSHIRE - EAST RIDING 1851
EYF = East Yorkshire FHS   * = Microfilm held
REGISTRATION DISTRICT   HO 107   Volume   Location
Beverley RD
- South Cave & Bevereley SDs
  (Excluding Beverley town)   2359* [ff4-241]   EYF 4   YK/C 43
Bridlington RD - Bridlington Quay   2367* [ff80-258] EYF 1   YK/C 15
Bridlington RD
- Skipton/Bridlington *part* &
  Hunmanby SDs   2367*[ff4-76,262-480] EYF 3   YK/C 42
Driffield RD
- Foston/Driffield SDs   2366*[ff4-381]   EYF 1   YK/C 15
- Bainton/Langtoft SDs   2366*[ff385-650]   EYF 4   YK/C 43
Howden RD   2358*   EYF 4   YK/C 43
Patrington RD   2364*   EYF 1   YK/C 15
Pocklington RD   2357*
Sculcoates RD
- Sutton on Hull SD   2360 *[ff4-245]   EYF 4   YK/C 43
- Cottingham North etc   2360 *[ff246-520]   EYF 4   YK/C 43
- Hedon, Drypool etc
  (inc Hull Garrison)   2360* [ff521-751]   EYF 4   YK/C 43
- Sculcoates East & West   2361* [ff4-725]   EYF 3   YK/C 42
- Hull Holy Trinity (part 3)   2362*   EYF 2   YK/C 39
- Hull Holy Trinity (part 1)   2363*   EYF 1   YK/C 15
- Hull Holy Trinity (part 2)   2363*   EYF 2   YK/C 39
Skirlaugh RD   2365*   EYF 3   YK/C 42
York RD   2353-2355*
- Skelton & Bootham SDs   2353*
- Micklegate SD   2354*
- Walmgate SD   2355*
- Escrick/Dunnington & Flaxton SDs 2356*
- Naburn/Escrick/Dunnington parishes 2356* [ff 4-157] EYF 3   YK/C 42
- Kexby tp (in Catton parish) 2356   YK/C 48

75

YORKSHIRE - EAST RIDING 1861 * = Microfilm held
REGISTRATION DISTRICT RG 9
Beverley RD 3567-3573*
Bridlington RD 3611-3614*
Driffield RD
 - Foston SD 3606,
 - Driffield part/Bainton & Langtoft SDs 3608-3610
Howden RD 3652-3566*
Hull RD 3587-3579*
Patrington RD 3598-3600*
Pocklington RD 3574-3586*
Sculcoates RD 3574-3586*
Skirlaugh RD 3601-3605*
York RD 3543-3557*

YORKSHIRE - EAST RIDING 1881
GSU Transcript & Indexes - county complete [Lower Library Mfc]

YORKSHIRE - EAST RIDING 1891
Lincolnshire FHS 1891 Census Index of Yorkshire [LIF]
REGISTRATION DISTRICT RG 12 Volume Location
Hull RD 3934-3937 LIF Mfc
Sculcoates RD 3912-3917 LIF Mfc

YORKSHIRE - NORTH RIDING (YK NR)

1811 Kilburn, South Otterington, Middleton [YK/C 53]
1811 Thirsk [YK/C 54]
1821 Thirsk [YK/C 54]
1821 Oswaldkirk [YK/C 53]
1821 Castle Bolton [YK/C 53]
1841 Bowes [YK/C 38]
1851-1881 Whenby village [YK/C 7]

YORKSHIRE - NORTH RIDING 1851
EYF = East Yorkshire FHS; CYF = Cleveland FHS: * = Microfilm held
REGISTRATION DISTRICT HO 107 Volume Location
Askrigg RD 2380*
 - Aysgath, Carperby & Thoresby, Burton
   cum Walden, Newbiggin, Bishopsdale 2380 CYF 94a YK/C 26
 - Thoralby, Thornton Rust, Bainbridge 2380 CYF 94b YK/C 26
 - Askrigg, Abbotside, Burtersett 2380 CYF 95 YK/C 26
 - Reeth, Heelaugh, Raw & Castle,
   Fremington, Whitaside, Harkerside,
   Grinton 2380 CYF 96 YK/C 26
 - Arkengarthdale, Hurst, Marrick,
   Ellerton Abbey 2380 CYF 97 YK/C 26
 - Gayle, Hawes, Appersett 2380 CYF 98 YK/C 26
 - Thorns & Keld, Stonesdale & Birkdale,
   Angram & Agill, Thwaite, Muker, Oxnop
   & Satron, Ivelet 2380 CYF 99 YK/C 26
 - Gunnerside, Lodge Green, Melbecks,
   Low Row, Kearton, Feetham 2380 CYF100 YK/C 26

Bedale RD	**2378**		
- Killerby, Kirby Fleetham, Fencote, Ainderby cum Holtby, Hackforth, Scriton, Firby	2378	CYF 85	YK/C 25
- Bedale SD	2378	CYF 86	YK/C 25
- Gatenby, Swainby, Theakston, Burneston, Carthorpe, Kirklington	2378	CYF 87	YK/C 25
- Well, Snape, Thornton Watlass	2378	CYF 88	YK/C 25
- Fireby, Langthorn, Leemung & Newton, Londonderry, Exelby	2378	CYF 101	YK/C 27
- Masham, Swinton, Ilton cum Post	2378	CYF 102	YK/C 27
- Crakedale, Aiskew & Leeming Bar	2378	CYF 103	YK/C 27
Easingwold RD	**2370**		
Guisborough RD	**2375**	CYF	Mfc
- Easington & Brotton, Skelton, Loftus, Kirkleatham & Upleatham, Redcar & Marske	2375	CYF 5 - 9	YK/C 1
- Wilton, Ormesby, Cleveland Port, Eston, Normanby	2375	CYF 13	YK/C 2
- Guisborough (inc Hutton Lowcross, Morton, Newton, Pinchinthorpe, Tockets, Upsall)	2375	CYF 18	YK/C 2
- Commondale, Castleton, Danby, Westerdale	2375	CYF 23	YK/C 10
Helmsley RD	**2372**	CYF	Mfc
- Arden inc Ardenside, Beadlam, Bilsdale Midcable, Bilsdale (West Side), Dale-Town, Hawnby, Helmsley, Laskill-Pasture, Morton (extra parochial), Old Bylands, Rievaulx, Snilesworth, Carlton	2372	CYF 89	YK/C 25
- Pockley, Harum, Sproxton, Scawton & Cold Kirby, Oldstead & Wass, Thorp le Willows, Byland Abbey, Ampleforth, Birdforth, Oswaldkirk, West Newton Grange	2372	CYF 90	YK/C 25
- Cawton & Grimston, Coulton, E. Ness & Nunnington, Gt & Lt Edstone, N. Holme, Gilling, E. Muscoats & Wilburn, Normanby & Thornton Risborough, Salton, Stonegrave & E. Newton, Wombleton	2372	CYF 91	YK/C 26
- Nawton, Brandale & Skiplam, Farndale Low Quarter, Farndale E & W Side, Gillamoor, Fadmoor, Hutton le Hole	2372	CYF 92	YK/C 26
- Kirbymoorside, Appleton le Moor	2372	CYF 93	YK/C 26
Leyburn RD	**2379**		
- Healey & Sutton, Fearby, Ellington, Ellingstring, E. Witton, Colsterdale,	2379	CYF 104	YK/C 27
- Middleham	2379	CYF 105	YK/C 27
- E & W Layton, Newsham, Carkin, Caldwell Forcett	2379	CYF 106	YK/C 27
- Coverham, Caldbergh, W Scrafton, Carlton (Highdale), Melmberby	2379	CYF 107	YK/C 27
- Wensley, Preston, Redmire, Castle Bolton, Leyburn	2379	CYF 108	YK/C 27
- Spennithorne, Bellerby, Hawkswell, Garriston with Barden, Hornby, Hunton, Patrick Brompton & Arrathorne	2379	CYF 109	YK/C 27
- Newton le Willows, Burrell, Burton on Ire,			

Thirn, Thornton Steward, Fingall, Constable Burton	2379	CYF 110	YK/C 27
Malton RD	**2369**		
Northallerton RD	**2377**		
- Deighton, E. & W. Harsley, E. & S. Cowton, Birkby, Hutton Bonvillle, Little Smeaton	2377	CYF 21	YK/C 10
- Northallerton & Romanby	2377	CYF 24	YK/C 10
- Ellerbeck, Nether & Over Silton, Thimbleby, Osmotherly	2377	CYF 35	YK/C 10
- Brompton (N'Allerton), Kirby Sigston, Thornton le Beans	2377	CYF 39	YK/C 11
- Landmoth with Catto & Gueldable, Borrowby, Crosby, Leake (ex. parochial), Cotcliffe (ex.parochial), Sowerby u Cotcliffe, Winston & Stank, N. Otterington & Warlaby	2377	CYF 54	YK/C 18
- Ainderby Steeple, Morton on Swale, Thrintoft, Yafforth, Danby Wiske with Lazenby, Gt & Lt Langton, Whitwell, Kiplin	2377	CYF 62	YK/C 19
Pickering RD	**2373**	CYF	Mfc
- Pickering SD	2373	CYF 112	YK/C 47
- Lastingham, Rosedale E. & W., Cropton, Hartoft, Cawthorne, Aislaby, Middleton	2373	CYF 116	YK/C 47
- Newton, Marishes, Sinnington, Marton, Kirby Misterton, Great & Little Barugh, Thornton Dale,	2373	CYF 117	YK/C 47
- Farmanby, Wilton, Allerston, Ebberston, Lockton, Levisham	2373	CYF 118	YK/C 47
Richmond RD	**2381**		
- Richmond SD	2381	CYF 57	YK/C 18
- Downholme, Stainton, Walburn, Marske, Hudswell, Hipswell, Easby & Aske	2381	CYF 70	YK/C 24
- Skeeby, Gilling, Hartford, Gatherley Moor, Sedbury	2381	CYF 71	YK/C 24
- Catterick, Brough, Scotton, Colburn, Tunstall, Appleton, Ellerton, Bolton on Swale, Scorton	2381	CYF 72	YK/C 24
- Middleton Tyas, N. Cowton, Moulton, Uckerby, Brompton on Swale	2381	CYF 77	YK/C 24
- Aldborough & Stanwick, Eppleby, Melsonby	2381	CYF 78	YK/C 24
- Kirby Hill with Washton, Ravensworth, Gales, New Forest	2381	CYF 81	YK/C 25
Scarborough RD	**2368**		
- excl Town (ff1-125, 512-836)	2368	EYF	YK/C 39
- Scarborough Town (ff 129-509)	2368	EYF 2	YK/C 39
Stokesley	**2376**		
- Great & Little Ayton	2376	CYF 10	YK/C 1
- E. & W. Rounton, Welbury, Appleton on Wiske, Hornby, Gt Smeaton	2376	CYF 15	YK/C 2
- Hemlington, Hilton, Marton, Nunthorpe, Tollesby	2376	CYF 19	YK/C 2
- Stokesley SD	2376	CYF 25	YK/C 10
- Faceby, Seamer, Sexhow, Potto, Crathorne, Hutton Radby, Middleton on Leven, Ingleby Arncliffe, Ingleby Cross,	2376	CYF 26	YK/C 10
- Newby, Easby, Carlton, Kildale,Whorlton	2376	CYF 29	YK/C 10
- Ingleby Greenhow, Battersby, Kirby &			

Dormanby, Great & Little Busby, Skutterskelfe, Gt & Lt Broughton	2376	CYF 40	YK/C 11
Thirsk RD	2371	CYF	Mfc
- Thirsk SD	2371	CYF 55	YK/C 18
- Thornton le Street, Thornton le Moor, N. Kilvington, Knayton, Kepwick, Cowesby	2371	CYF 56	YK/C 18
- Ainderby Quernhow, Catton, Sinderby, Skipton, Howe, Holme, Pickhill with Roxby	2371	CYF 59	YK/C 18
- Hutton Sessay, Birdforth, Sessay, Dalton, Eldmire, Fawdington, Topcliffe	2371	CYF 63	YK/C 18
- Sowerby	2371	CYF 64	YK/C 19
- S. Kilvington, Bagby, Sutton with Balk, Thirkleby	2371	CYF 65	YK/C 19
- Kilburn, Felixkirk, Thirlby, Boltby, Upsall, Thornborough, Kirby Knowle	2371	CYF 67	YK/C 19
- Maunby, Newby Wiske, S Otterington, Kirkby Wiske, Newsham cum Breckenborough, Carlton Miniott, Sandhutton	2371	CYF 68	YK/C 19
Whitby	2374		
- Fylingdales (inc Robin Hoods Bay)	2374	CYF 27	YK/C 10
- Hinderwell, Staithes, Roxby, Runswick Bay	2374	CYF 28	YK/C 10
- Barnby, Borrowby, Ellerby, Goldsborough, Mulgrave, Kettleness, Lythe, Mickleby, Sandsend, Ugthorpe	2374	CYF 31	YK/C 11
- Sleights, Eskdale, Glaisdale	2374	CYF 34	YK/C 11
- Ruswarp	2374	CYF 36	YK/C 11
- Whitby SD	2374	CYF 37 a&b	YK/C 11
- Egton, Ugglebarnby, Goathland	2374	CYF 38	YK/C 11
- Newholm cum Dunsley, Sneaton, Aislaby, Hawsker cum Stainsacre	2374	CYF 42	YK/C 17

YORKSHIRE - NORTH RIDING 1861
Fylingdales [YK/C 38]

* = Microfilm held

REGISTRATION DISTRICT	RG 9	REGISTRATION DISTRICT	RG 9
Easingwold RD	3629-3631*	**Richmond RD**	
Guisborough RD	3652-3656*	- Newsham/Aldborough SDs	3677-3678*
Helmsley RD	3637-3640*	**Scarborough RD**	
Malton RD	3623-3628*	- Filey/Scarborough *part* SDs	3615-3619
Northallerton RD	2660-3662*	**Stokelsey RD**	3657-3659*
Pickering RD	3641-3645*	**Thirsk RD**	3632-3636*

YORKSHIRE - NORTH RIDING 1877
Leeming Bar [YK/C 53]

YORKSHIRE - NORTH RIDING 1881
GSU Transcript & Indexes - county complete [Lower Library Mfc]

YORKSHIRE - NORTH RIDING 1891
Cleveland FHs 1891 Census Index [CYF].

* = Microfilm held

REGISTRATION DISTRICT	RG 12	Volume	Location
Middlesborough RD	4004-4021		
- Southbank/Eston Junction/Grangetown	4015-4017	CYF	Mfc
Richmond RD - Aldborough SD *part*	4039*		

Whitby RD
- Whitby & Ruswarp   3994-3995   CYF   Mfc
- Whitby SD (villages)   3995   CYF   Mfc

YORKSHIRE - WEST RIDING (YKWR)

1723 Wakefield communicants & souls [YK/C 54]
1764 Methley [SP 79/15]
1767 YK papist returns (*in 2 vols*) (CRS Occ Papers 1 & 2) [RC/PER]
1776 Wetherby population list [YK/C 54]
1780 Bradford (Westgate) [YK/C 54]
1801 Bracewell tp [YK/C 52]
Elland cum Greetland [YK/C 12]
Langfield [YK/C 12]
Leeds [YK/C 54]
Midgley cens [YK/C 12]
Spofforth tp [YK/C 52]
Tong tp [YK/C 53]
1804 Bradford [YK/C 54]
Little Horton [YK/C 54]
1811 Calverley & Farsley tps [YK/C 52]
Carlton in Craven [YK/C 53]
Elland cum Greatland tp [YK/C 52]
Midgley [YK/C 12 & 52]
Sowerby cens [YK/C 12 & 52]]
Tong [YK/C 53]
Yeadon tp [YK/C 53]

1821 Spofforth tp [TK/C 52]
Tong tp [YK/C 53]
Yeadon [YK/C 53]
1831 Potternewton & Chapel Allerton census (Mfc) [Apply to Staff]
Spofforth tp [YK/C 52]
Stansfield [YK/C C54]
Yeadon [YK/C 53]
1841 Ardsley [YK/C 48]
Burley & Poole tps [YK/C 52]
Clayton tp [YK/C 52]
Clifton cum Hartshead chap [YK/C 52]
Eccleshill tp YK/C 54]
Essholt
Fixby [YK/C 38]
Hawkesworth tp [YK/C 52]
Heckmondwick tp YK/C 52]
Hunsworth tp [YK/C 53]
Ilkley [YK/C 52]
Menston tp [TK/C 52]
Otley tp [YK/C 52]
Tong tp [YK/C 53]
Wetherby tp [YK/C 53]

YORKSHIRE - WEST RIDING **1841-1861**
Walton [YK/C 48]

YORKSHIRE - WEST RIDING **1851**
BAF = Barnsley FHS area indexes; CDF = Calderdale FHS Indexes; DON = Doncaster & District FHS Archdeaconry of Doncaster area indexes; HUF = Huddersfield & District FHS Kirklees area indexes; NTF = Nottinghamshire FHS Census Indexes; RHS = Ripon, Harrogate & District FHS: WDF= Wakefield FHS indexes; WFH = Wharfedale FHS; YAS = Yorkshire Archaeological Society FHS Occasional Papers   * = Microfilm held

REGISTRATION DISTRICT	HO 107	Volume	Location
Barnsley RD	2332-2333*		
- Monk Bretton	2332	BAF11	YK/C 55
- Darfield	2333	BAF 9	YK/C 55
Bradford RD	2303-2313*		
- Calverley, Farsley & Pudsey	2313	YAS 5	Mfc
Dewsbury RD	2322-2325*		
- Batley	2322	HUF 1	YK/C28
- Morley & Batley	2322	YAS 11	Mfc
- Kirklees area	2323-2325pt HUF		YK/C 28 - 33

- Gomersall	2323	HUF 3	YK/C 30
- Heckmondwicke	2323	HUF 3	YK/C 30
- Liversedge	2323	HUF 5	YK/C 32
- Dewsbury	2324	HUF 2	YK/C 29
- Mirfield	2324	HUF 5	YK/C 32
- Soothill	2325	HUF 6	YK/C 33
- Thornhill	2325	HUF 6	YK/C 33
- Whitley, Upper & Lower	2325	HUF 6	YK/C 33
Doncaster RD	2346-2348		YK/C 3, 21, 23, 46
Doncaster RD	2438	NTF 9	NT/C 1 - 2
- Burghwallis, Haywood, Skelbroke, Hampole, Adwick le Street & Brodsworth	2346*	DON 15	YK/C 21
- High Melton, Barnborough, Sprotborough, Cadeby & Cusworth	2346*	DON 16	YK/C 21
- Hickleton, Hooton Pagnall, Clayton with Frickley, Marr & Pickburn	2346*	DON 17	YK/C 21
- Balby with Hexthorpe & Warmsworth	2346*	DON 22	YK/C 21
- Mexbrough	2346*	DON 24	YK/C 21
- Tickhill, Wilsick, Stancil & Wellingley	2346*	DON 26	YK/C 23
- Conisborough	2346*	DON 42	YK/C 46
- Doncaster	2347*	DON 12 - 14	YK/C 3
- Kirk Bramwith, Fenwick & Moss	2348	DON 1	YK/C 3
- Burghwallis, Haywood, Skelbroke, Hampole, Adwick le Street & Brodsworth	2348	DON 15	YK/C 21
- Wasdsworth, Edlington & Rossington	2348	DON 18	YK/C 21
- Norton & Campsell	2348	DON 2	YK/C 3
- Askern, Sutton Owston, Skellow & Wheatley	2348	DON 3	YK/C 3
- Thorpe in Balne, Barnby Dun, Kirk Sandall & Wheatley	2348	DON 6	YK/C 3
Ecclesall Bierlow RD	2336-2337		
Goole RD	2350*		
- Goole	2350	DON 39 - 40	YK/C 46
- Pollington & Cowick	2350	DON 19	YK/C 21
- Snaith & Gowdall	2350	DON 21	YK/C 21
- Ousefleet, Reedness & Whitgift	2350	DON 33	YK/C 23
- Swinefleet	2350	DON 34	YK/C 23
- Hook	2350	DON 43	YK/C 51
- Airmin & Rawcliffe	2350	DON 46	YK/C 51
Halifax RD	2297-2302		
- Rastrick/Brighouse & Southowram SDs	2297*		
- Halifax SD	2298*		
- Elland/Ripondale SDs	2299		
- Sowerby/Cuddenden SDs	2300		
- Ovenden SD	2301		
- Northowram SD	2302*		
- Hartshead cum Clifton	2297	HUF 3	YK/C 30
- Cleckheaton	2303	HUF 1	YK/C 28
- Hunsworth	2303	HUF 4	YK/C 31
Hemsworth RD	2331*		
Huddersfield RD - Kirklees area	2291-2296*	HUF	YK/C 28 - 33
- Almondbury	2294	HUF 1	YK/C 28
- Austonley	2292	HUF 1	YK/C 28
- Cartworth	2292	HUF 1	YK/C 28

- Crossland, South	2291	HUF 2	YK/C 29
- Cumberworth & Cumberworth Half	2293	HUF 2	YK/C 29
- Dalton	2294	HUF 2	YK/C 29
- Farnley Tyas	2294	HUF 3	YK/C 30
- Fulstone	2293	HUF 3	YK/C 30
- Golcar	2296	HUF 3	YK/C 30
- Hepworth	2293	HUF 3	YK/C 30
- Holme	2292	HUF 3	YK/C 30
- Honley	2292	HUF 4	YK/C 31
- Huddersfield SD	2295	HUF	YK/C 37
- Kirkburton	2293	HUF 4	YK/C 31
- Kirkheaton	2294	HUF 4	YK/C 31
- Lepton	2294	HUF 4	YK/C 31
- Lindley cum Quarmby	2296	HUF 4	YK/C 31
- Linthwaite *part*	2291	HUF 4	YK/C 31
- Linthwaite *part*	2296	HUF 4	YK/C 31
- Lockwood	2296	HUF 5	YK/C 32
- Longwood	2296	HUF 5	YK/C 32
- Marsden	2291	HUF 5	YK/C 32
- Meltham	2291	HUF 5	YK/C 32
- Netherthong	2292	HUF 6	YK/C 33
- Scammondon	2296	HUF 6	YK/C 33
- Shelley	2293	HUF 6	YK/C 33
- Shepley	2293	HUF 6	YK/C 33
- Slaithwaite	2291	HUF 6	YK/C 33
- Thurstonland	2293	HUF 6	YK/C 33
- Upperthong	2292	HUF 6	YK/C 33
- Wooldale *part*	2292	HUF 6	YK/C 33
Hunslet RD	2314-2318*		
- Wortley, Farnley, Armley & Gildersome	2314	YAS 8	Mfc
- Bramley, Stanningley [ff 1-281]	2315	YAS 12	Mfc
- Headingley cum Burle [ff284-397]	2315	YAS 16	Mfc
- Kirkstall [ff 401-473]	2315	YAS 18	Mfc
- Horsforth [ff477-618]	2315	YAS 15	Mfc
- Potternewton, Chapel Allerton [ff4-132]	2316	YAS 17	Mfc
- Shadwell, Roundhay, Seacroft [ff136-211]	2316	YAS 21	Mfc
- Austhorpe, Whitkirk, Halton [ff 215-308]	2316	YAS 23	Mfc
- Rothwell [ff 323-508]	2316	YAS 22	Mfc
- Holbeck, Beeston, Churwell	2317	YAS 6	Mfc
- Hunslet SD	2318	YAS 10	Mfc
Keighley RD	2286-2287*		
Knaresborough RD	2282-2283*		
- Knaresborough [ff1-443]	2282	RHS 1-3	YK/C 44
- Knaresborough [ff 231-614]	2283	RHS 6-7	YK/C 44
Leeds RD	2319-2321*	YAS 3-4	YK/C 8 - 9
Otley RD	2284-2285*		
- complete (except Otley town)	2284	WFH	YK/C 58
- Baildon, Esholt & Hawksworth [ff 290-407]	2285	YAS 14	Mfc
- Guisley with Carlton [ff 1-90]	2285	YAS 13	Mfc
- Harewood SD	2284		YK/C 5
- Rawden [ff 212-286]	2285	YAS 20	Mfc
- Yeadon [ff92-208]	2285	YAS 19	Mfc
Pateley Bridge RD	2280		
Pontefract RD	2329-2330*		YK/C 23, 46
- Ferrybridge, Ferry Fryston	2329	DON 36	YK/C 46

- Knottingley	2329	DON 37 - 38	YK/C 46
- Beal, Kellington, Eggborough, Whitley Bridge	2329	DON 44	YK/C 51
- Hensall, Heck, Balne	2329	DON 45	YK/C 51
- Castlford	2330	DON 35	YK/C 46
- Pontefract	2330	DON 29 - 31	YK/C 23
- Carleton, Darrington, East Hardwick & Stapleton	2330	DON 27	YK/C 23
- Adlingfleet, Eastoft, Fockerby, Garthorpe, Haldenby, Luddington	2330	DON 28	YK/C 23
Ripon RD	**2281**		
Rotherham RD	**2343-2345***		
- Swinton	2345	DON 4	YK/C3
- Wath upon Dearne	2345	DON 41	YK/C 46
- Wentworth	2345	DON 5	YK/C3
Saddleworth RD	**2290***		
Sedburgh RD	**2276**		
Selby RD	**2351**		
Settle RD	**2277**		
Settle parish			YK/C 38
Sheffield RD	**2338-2342**		
Skipton RD	**2278-2279**		
Tadcaster RD	**2352**		
- Acaster, Selby, Appleton, Roebuck, Bolton Percy, Kirk Fenton, Little Fenton, Barkston, Sherburn	2352	YAS 26	Mfc
- Aberford, Barwick in Elmet etc	2352	YAS 24	Mfc
-Thorner, Scarcroft, Bardsley, East Keswick, Clifford, Boston etc	2352	YAS 25	Mfc
- Bramham, Thorp Arch, Newton Kyme, Ulleskelf, Kirkby Wharf, Stutton Healaugh, Wighill	2352	YAS 27	Mfc
- Tadcaster, Bilbrough, Bickerton Bilton, Tockwith, Long Merton	2352	YAS 28	Mfc
Thorne RD	**2349**		
- Thorne	2349	DON 10 - 11	YK/C 3
- Hatfield	2349	DON 20	YK/C 21
- Stainforth	2349	DON 23	YK/C 21
- Fishlake & Skyhouse	2349	DON 25	YK/C 23
Todmorden RD	**2289**		
- Hebden Bridge SD	2288	CDF	Mfc
- Todmorden SD	2288	CDF	Mfc
Wakefield RD	**2326-2328***		
- Emley	2326	HUF 2	YK/C 29
- Floxton	2326	HUF 3	YK/C 30
- Wakefield SD	2327	WDF 1 - 8	YK/C 56
Wortley RD	**2334-2335**		
- Clayton, West	2334	HUF 1	YK/C28
- Denby	2334	HUF 2	YK/C 29
- Silkstone	2234	BAF 1	YK/C 55
- Thurgoland & Cranemoor	2234	BAF 2	YK/C 55
- Cawthorne	2234	BAF 4	YK/C 55
- Kexborough	2234	BAF 5	YK/C 55
- Oxspring & Hunshelf	2234	BAF 6	YK/C 55
- Tankersley & Pilley	2234	BAF 7	YK/C 55
- Hoylandswaine, Gunthwaite & Ingbirchworth	2234	BAF 8	YK/C 55

- Thurlston	2234	BAF 12	YK/C 55
Worksop RD - Yorkshire part	2122	NTF 9	NT/C 1-2

YORKSHIRE - WEST RIDING 1861   * = Microfilm held

REGISTRATION DISTRICT	RG 9	REGISTRATION DISTRICT	RG 9
Barnsley RD	3442-3452*	Otley RD	3211-3215*
Bradford RD	3305-3348*	Pateley Bridge RD	3192-3195*
Dewsbury RD	3397-3416*	Pontefract RD	3431-3439*
Doncaster RD	3513-3522*	Ripon RD	3196-3200*
Ecclesall Bierlow RD	3462-3475*	Rotherham RD	3502-3512*
Goole RD	3527-3530*	Saddleworth RD	3238-3242*
Great Ouseburn RD	3201-3203*	Sedburgh RD	3531-3535
Halifax RD		Selby RD	3531-3535*
- Rastrick/Brighouse/		Settle RD	3177-3181*
Southowram/Halifax SDs	3274-3285*	Sheffield RD	3476-3501*
- Luddenden/Ovenden &		Skipton RD	3182-3191*
Northowram SDs	3295-3304*	Tadcaster RD	3536-3542*
Hemsworth RD	3440-3441*	Thorne RD	3523-3526*
Huddersfield RD	3243-3273*	Todmorden RD	3230-3237*
Hunslet RD	3349-3369*	Wakefield RD	3417-3430*
Keighley RD	3219-3229*	Wharfedale RD	3216-3218*
Kirk Deighton RD	3210*	Wortley RD	3453-3461*
Knaresborough RD	3204-3207*		
Leeds RD	3370-3396*		

YORKSHIRE - WEST RIDING 1861
Sheffield FHS 1861 Census Index [YSF]; Nottinghamshire FHS Census Indexes [NTF]

REGISTRATION DISTRICT	RG 9	Volume	Location
Bradfield Chapelry (pts 1&2)	3460-3461	YSF	Shelf 9
Doncaster RD			
- Tickhill SD	3513	YSF 42	Mfc
- Yorkshire part	3522	NTF 41	NT/C 5
Ecclesall Bierlow RD			
- Nether & Upper Hallam SDs	3462-3466	YSF 28-32	Mfc
- Norton, Ecclesall Bierlow SDs	3467-3495	YSF 33-41	Mfc
Sheffield RD			
- Sheffield SD	3476-3479	YSF 1-4	YK/C 13
- Sheffield West SD	3480-3486	YSF 5-11	YK/C 22
- Sheffield South SD	3487-3489	YSF 12-14	Mfc
- Sheffield Park SD	3490-3493	YSF 15-18	Mfc
- Sheffield Brightside SD	3494-3499	YSF 19-24	Mfc
- Sheffield - Attercliffe cum Darnell, Handsworth, Beighton	3500-3502	YSF 25-27	Mfc
Rotherham RD			
- Rotherham/Kimberworth/Wath/Maltby SDs	3503-3512	YSF 45	Mfc
Worksop RD			
- Carlton/Anston SDs	2420-2421	YSF 45	Mfc
- Yorkshire part	2418-2422	NTF 41	NT/C 5
Wortley RD - Ecclesfield SD	3457-3459	YSF 42-44	Mfc

YORKSHIRE - WEST RIDING **1871**
Bradford & District FHS 1871 Census Index [BDF] (NB = North Brierley Union);
Nottinghamshire FHS Census Indexes [NTF]; WFH = Wharfedale FHS

REGISTRATION DISTRICT	RG 10	Volume	Location
Bradford RD			
- East End SD	4550-4562	BDF 1-2	Mfc
- West End SD	4363-4367	BDF 3-4	Mfc
- Horton SD	4468-4481	BDF 5	Mfc
- Manningham SD	4481-4487	BDF 5	Mfc
- Bowling SD	4443-4449	BDF 6	Mfc
Bradford RD (NB)			
- North Brierley SD	4438-4432	BDF 6	Mfc
- Thornton SD	4438-4432	BDF 7	Mfc
- Wilsden SD	4494-4496	BDF 7	Mfc
- Shipley SD	4497-4500	BDF 7	Mfc
- Idle SD	4501-4504	BDF 8	Mfc
- Calverley SD	4505	BDF 8	Mfc
- Pudsey SD	4506-4500	BDF 8	Mfc
- Cleckheaton SD	4430-4434	BDF 9	Mfc
- Drighlinghton SD	4435-4437	BDF 9	Mfc
Doncaster RD *part*	4723	NTF 67	NT/C 7
Hunslet RD - Horsforth tp	4298-4299	WFH	YK/C 58
Worksop RD - Yorkshire part	3458-3463	NTF 68	NT/C 7

YORKSHIRE - WEST RIDING **1881**
GSU Transcript & Indexes - county complete [Lower Library Mfc]

YORKSHIRE - WEST RIDING **1891**
Bradford & District FHS 1891 Census Index [BDF]; Nottinghamshire FHS 1851 Census Indexes [NTF]

REGISTRATION DISTRICT	RG 12	Volume	Location
Bradford RD	3620-3610		
- Bradford East & West SDs	3620-3636	BDF 1-4	YK/C 34
- Horton SD	3637-3643	BDF 5-6	YK/C 34
- Bowling, Birling SD *part*	3615-3619	BDF 7	YK/C 34
- North Bierley, Thornton & Wilsden SDs 3613-3614		BDF 8	YK/C 34
- Idle & Shipley SDs	3651-3653	BDF 9	YK/C 34
- Calverley & Pudsey SDs	3654-3655	BDF 10	YK/C 34
- Cleckheaton & Drighlington SDs	3608-3610	BDF 11	YK/C 34
Doncaster RD *part*	3857	NTF 85/6	NT/C 9
Leeds RD (Jewish Residents only)			YK/C 45
Worksop RD - Yorkshire part	2643-2647	NTF 85/6	NT/C 9

CHANNEL ISLANDS (CI)

CHANNEL ISLANDS - JERSEY (JER)   * = Microfilm held
1737 St Clement's list (*males 16-20*) (CI FH J 53) [CI/PER]
1750 JER French prot list (CI FH J 3/38) [CI/PER]
1788 St Lawrence (CI FH J 1/8-14) [CI/PER]
1849 JER 'Godfray' svy (*exc St Helier, St Aubin, Beaumont & Gorey*) (CI FH J 2/17) [CI/PER]

CHANNEL ISLANDS - JERSEY 1851
Channel Islands FHS 1851 Census Index HO 107/2527-2529 [CI/C 2]

CHANNEL ISLANDS - **1861** - ALDERNEY, JERSEY & GUERNSEY RG/9 4374-4408*

CHANNEL ISLANDS - **1881** - ALDERNEY, GUERNSEY, JERSEY & SARK
GSU Transcript & Indexes - county complete [Lower Library Mfc]

CHANNEL ISLANDS - **1891** JERSEY
Channel Islands FHS 1891 Census Index RG 12/4693-4700 [CI/C 1]

ISLE OF MAN (IM)

c1757   Castletown census (*Fraueyn as Banglaneyan* 15/4-16/2) [IM/PER]
c1820   Braddan (Kirk) census (*Fraueyn as Banglaneyan* 17/2) [IM/PER]

ISLE OF MAN **1851**   HO 107 2523-2526   No microfilms held
Isle of Man FHS 1851 Census Indexes cover following parishes:

PARISH	Location	PARISH	Location
Andreas	IM/C 6	(Kirk) Marown	IM/C 7
Arbory	IM/C 6	Maughold	IM/C 7
Ballagh	IM/C 6	Michael	IM/C 7
Braddan	IM/C 6	Onchin	IM/C 8
(Kirk) Bride	IM/C 6	(Kirk) Patrick	IM/C 8
Douglas	IM/C 6 or 1	Peel	IM/C 8 or 3
German	IM/C 6	Ramsey	IM/C 8
Jurby	IM/C 6	Rushen	IM/C 8
Lezayre	IM/C 7 or 2	(Kirk) Santen	IM/C 8
Lonan	IM/C 7	(Kirk) Bride 1851-1881	IM/C5
Malew & Castletown	IM/C 7		

ISLE OF MAN **1861**   All microfilms held

PARISH	RG 9		
Andreas	4410	Lonan	4423
Arbory	4409	Malew	4414 *part*, 4424 *part*
Ballaugh	4411	Marowen	4426
Braddan	4412, 4417-4419	Maughold	4425
Bride	4413	Michael	4431
Conchan *see* Onchan		Onchan	4415-4416
Douglas	4416	Onchan	4427
German	4420	Patrick	4427
Jurby	4421	Peel	4429
Lezayre	4422	Rushen	4430
		St Ann	4432

ISLE OF MAN **1881**
GSU Transcript & Indexes - county complete [Lower Library Mfc]

ISLE OF MAN **1891**
Isle of Man FHS 1891 Census Indexes cover following parishes:

PARISH	RG 12 Location		Lonan	4686	IM/C 5
Andreas	4684	IM/C 5	Malew	4691	IM/C 5
Ballaugh	4684	IM/C 5	Marowen	4683	IM/C 5
Braddan	4687	IM/C 5	Maughold	4684-85	IM/C 5
Braddan - St Anne	4690	IM/C 5	Michael	4683	IM/C 5
Bride	4684	IM/C 5	Onchan	4686-88	IM/C 5
Douglas	4687-89	IM/C 5	Patrick	4682	IM/C 5
German	4682-83	IM/C 5	Peel	4683	IM/C 5
Jurby	4684	IM/C 5	Ramsey	4685	IM/C 5
Lezayre	4684-85	IM/C 5	Rushen	4692	IM/C 5

ROYAL NAVY at sea & in ports abroad **1861**   RG 12/4433-4441*

IRELAND (IR)

Note: *apart from a few isolated exceptions few pre-1901 censuses have survived; but see "Tracing your Irish Ancestors" by John Greenham [TB Quick Ref] for lists of substitutes, many of which are held by the Library; in addition to censuses, the following lists the Library's holdings of* **Griffith's Primary Valuation ("GPV")** *returns made between 1848 and 1864,* **Protestant Returns** *(which often include non-protestants) and a few surveys; the Library also holds a number of Irish Hearth Tax Rolls for 1662-89: see the Library's Main Catalogue for details*

Census of Ireland **1851** - General Alphabetical Index to the Townlands and Towns of Ireland [TB Quick Ref]
Census of Ireland **1871** - Alphabetical Index to the Townlands & Towns of Ireland [IR/C 1]
1766 Religious Census of Ireland [IR/G 182]

Co ANTRIM (ANT)
c**1659** ANT census [IR/C 3]
1803 Ballintoy census ext (Ir Heritage Links 5/10) [IR/PER]
1804-10 Ballymoney list (N Ir Roots 2/3) [IR/PER]
1841 ANT OAP claims: census exts index (Mfc) [Apply to Staff]
1851 ANT OAP claims: census exts index (Mfc) [Apply to Staff]
1860 Belfast City GPV AIH index (Mfc) [Apply to Staff]; Belfast: St Anne's & Smithfield Wards GPV ret [IR/L 150 or exts (Ir Heritage Links 4/1-2) IR/PER]
1861-62 ANT GPV NLI index (*exc Belfast*) (Mfc) [Apply to Staff]

Co ARMAGH (ARM)
1602 The Fews census (Co LOU Archl J 8/2) [IR/PER]
1654-56 ARM civ svy exts (Analecta Hibernica 24) [IR/PER]
c**1659** ARM census [IR/C 3]
1766 Creggan prot census (Co LOU Archl J 8/2) [IR/PER]
1821 Kilmore: Derryhale census (N Ir Roots 3/1) [IR/PER]
1841 ARM OAP claims: census exts index (Mfc) [Apply to Staff]
1851 ARM OAP claims: census exts index (Mfc) [Apply to Staff]

1864 ARM GPV NLI index (Mfc) [Apply to Staff]

Co CARLOW (CAR)
c1659 CAR census [IR/C 3]
1852 CAR GPV AIH index (Mfc) [Apply to Staff]
1852-53 CAR GPV NLI index (Mfc) [Apply to Staff]

Co CAVAN (CAV)
c1802 CAV Meath Diocese prot ret (Ir Ancestor 5/2) [IR/PER]
1814 Drung & Larah prot rets ext (children) (Ir Ancestor 10/1) [IR/PER]
1821 Lurgan, Mullagh & Munterconnaught cens [Mf 1789]
1841 Killashandra census [Mf 1793]
1854 Kells Union GPV ret [IR/L 4]
1855 Granard Union GPV ret [IR/L 156]
1856 Bailieborough Union GPV ret [IR/L 1]
1856-57 CAV GPV NLI index (Mfc) [Apply to Staff]
1857 Cavan Union GPV ret [IR/L 2]

Co CLARE (CLA)
1641 CLA svy & distrbn [IR/G 172]
c1659 CLA census [IR/C 3]
1855 CLA GPV NLI index (Mfc) [Apply to Staff]; Scarriff Union GPV ret [IR/L 6]

Co CORK (CO)
c1659 CO census [IR/C 3]
1766 Kilmichael prot census (J CO Hist & Archl Soc 2nd 26/2-27/1) [IR/PER]
1851-53 CO GPV NLI index (Mfc *in 3 ridings*) [Apply to Staff]
1852 CO GPV ret (Mfc); CO GPV AIH index (Mfc) [*both:* APPLY TO STAFF]

Co DERRY: *see Co Londonderry*

Co DONEGAL (DON)
1654 DON civ svy [IR/G 17]
c1659 DON census [IR/C 3]
1740 Glendermot prot census [IR/G 124]
1799 Templecrone prot ret (Ir Ancestor 16/2) [IR/PER]
1841 DON OAP claims: census exts index (Mfc) [Apply to Staff]
1851 DON OAP claims: census exts index (Mfc) [Apply to Staff]
1857 DON GPV NLI index (Mfc) [Apply to Staff]
1858 DON GPV ret (Mfc) [Apply to Staff]

Co DOWN (DOW)
see Co Antrim for Belfast
c1659 DOW census [IR/C 3]
1841 DOW OAP claims: census exts index (Mfc) [Apply to Staff]
1851 DOW OAP claims: census exts index (Mfc) [Apply to Staff]; Loughisland: Clough Presbyterian census (Family Links 1/6-7) [IR/PER]
1861 Loughisland: Clough Presbyterian census (Family Links 1/6-7) [IR/PER]
1863-64 DOW GPV NLI index (Mfc) [Apply to Staff]

Co DUBLIN (DUB)
1641 Newcastle & Uppercross Barony svy & distrbn [IR/G 21]
c1650 Newcastle & Uppercross Barony census ext (Ir Gengst 7/4-8/4) [IR/PER]

1654-56 DUB civ svy (exc Dublin City, the Liberties & Newcastle & Uppercross Barony) [IR/G 21]
c1659 DUB census [IR/C 3]
1766 Crumlin prot census [IR/R 11]; Monkstown Union prot census [IR/R 26 or (Dun Laoghaire Gencal Soc J 1/4) IR/PER]
1841 Rathdown Barony OAP claims: census exts (Dun Laoghaire Gencal Soc J 5/1) [IR/PER]
1848 Dublin City: St Michael's GPV ret (Dun Laoghaire Gencal Soc J 4/3) [IR/PER]
1848-51 DUB GPV NLI index (exc Dublin city) (Mfc) [Apply to Staff]
1851 Newmarket: St Luke's census (Familia 2/2); Rathdown Barony OAP claims: census exts (Dun Laoghaire Gencal Soc J 5/1) [both IR/PER]
1854 Dublin City GPV AIH index (Mfc) [Apply to Staff]
1857 Taney GPV ret (Gateway to the Past 2/1) [IR/PER]
1911 Balinteer census (Gateway to the Past 1/5) [IR/PER]

Co FERMANAGH (FER)
c1659 FER census [IR/C 3]
1821 FER census ext; Aughalurcher census [both IR/L 29]
1841 FER OAP claims: census exts index (Mfc) [Apply to Staff]
1851 FER OAP claims: census exts index (Mfc) [Apply to Staff]
1862 FER GPV NLI index (Mfc); FER GPV AIH index (Mfc) [Apply to Staff for both]
1901 FER census (Mfc) [Apply to Staff]

Co GALWAY (GAL)
1641 GAL svy & distrbn [IR/L 95 or IR/G 171]
1821 GAL census ext (UT Gencal & Hist Mag 9/2) [US/UT/PER]
1834 Duras, Killina & Kinvara lists (GAL Roots 2) [IR/PER]
1851 Galway Town OAP claims: census exts (GAL Roots 4) [IR/PER]
1853-56 GAL GPV NLI index (Mfc) [Apply to Staff]
c1854 Aran Is GPV ret ext (surname frequency) (GAL Roots 3); Boughill GPV ret (GAL Roots 3); Irvalloughter GPV ret (GAL Roots 3) [all IR/PER]
1855 Scarriff Union GPV ret [IR/L 6]
1901 Boughill census (GAL Roots 3); Galway Town exts (St Helen's Orphanage & St Anne's Industrial School) (GAL Roots 4); Irvalloughter census (GAL Roots 3); Salthill census ext (Industrial School) (GAL Roots 4) [all IR/PER]

Co KERRY (KER)
1654 KER civ svy exts (Analecta Hibernica 24) [IR/PER]; Clanmaurice Barony (pt) civ svy [IR/G 18]
c1659 KER census [IR/C 3]
1852 KER GPV NLI index (Mfc) [Apply to Staff]

Co KILDARE (KLD)
1641 Offaly Barony svy & distrbn [IR/G 22]
1654 KLD civ svy (exc Offaly Barony) [IR/G 22]
c1659 KLD census [IR/C 3]
1850 Celbridge Union GPV ret [IR/L 3]; S Salt Barony GPV ret [IR/L 157]
1851 KLD GPV NLI index (Mfc) [Apply to Staff]

Co KILKENNY (KLK)
c1659 KLK census [IR/C 3]
1821 Aglish census (Ir Gengst 8/2); Iverk Barony census ext (Ir Gengst 5/3-5); Portnascully census (Ir Gengst 8/2) [all IR/PER]

1849-50 KLK GPV NLI index (Mfc) [Apply to Staff]
1841 Aglish census ext (Ir Ancestor 9/1) [IR/PER]
1851 Aglish census (Ir Ancestor 9/2) [IR/PER]
1901 Kilkenny Town: St John's, St Maul's, etc census exts [IR/L 158]; Kilkenny Town: St Patrick's census ext [IR/M 31]

KING'S Co (KIN)
c1659 KIN census [IR/C 3]
c1802 KIN Meath Diocese prot ret (Ir Ancestor 5/2) [IR/PER]
1854 KIN GPV NLI index (Mfc) [Apply to Staff]

Co LEITRIM (LTR)
c1659 LTR census [IR/C 3]
1856 LTR GPV NLI index (Mfc) [Apply to Staff]

Co LEIX/LAOIS: see Queen's Co

Co LIMERICK (LIM)
1654-56 LIM civ svy [IR/G 18]
c1659 LIM census [IR/C 3]
1766 LIM prot census ext (Ir Ancestor 9/2) [IR/PER]
1850 LIM GPV AIH index (Mfc) [Apply to Staff]
1851-52 LIM GPV NLI index (Mfc) [Apply to Staff]

Co LONDONDERRY (LND)
1628 Londonderry City census [IR/L 65]
1654-56 LND civ svy [IR/G 17]
c1659 LND census [IR/C 3]
1740 Banagher & Faughanvale prot cens [IR/G 124]
1766 Banagher prot census [IR/G 124]
1803 Faughanvale list (Ulster Gencal & Hist Guild N/L 1/10) [IR/PER]
1831 LND census [Mf 1789-93 or (Mfc) [Apply to Staff]; Aghanloo, Ballycastle & Tamlat Finlagan cens [IR/L 29]
1832 Londonderry City 1st valuation (*index*) [Apply to Staff (Shelf 9)]
1841 LND OAP claims: census exts index (Mfc) [Apply to Staff]
1851 LND OAP claims: census exts index (Mfc) [Apply to Staff]
1858 LND GPV ret (Mfc) [Apply to Staff]; Londonderry City 2nd valuation (*index*) [Apply to Staff (Shelf 9)]
1858-59 LND GPV NLI index (Mfc) [Apply to Staff]

Co LONGFORD (LNG)
1654-56 LNG civ svy exts (Analecta Hibernica 24) [IR/PER]
c1659 LNG census [IR/C 3]
1854 LNG GPV ret (Mfc); LNG GPV NLI index (Mfc); LNG GPV AIH index (Mfc) [Apply to Staff *for each*]
1901 LNG census [IR/C 2]; Longford Town census ext 1901 (A-ENG) (Ir Heritage Links 6/2) [IR/PER]

Co LOUTH (LOU)
1602 The Fews census (Co LOU Archl J 8/2) [IR/PER]
c1659 LOU census [IR/C 3]
1654-56 Louth Barony civ svy [IR/G 24]

1766 Creggan prot census (Co LOU Archl J 8/2) [IR/PER]; Dromiskin prot census [IR/L 58]
1821 Kilsaran Union census ext [IR/L 58]
1854 LOU GPV NLI index (Mfc) [Apply to Staff]

Co MAYO (MAY)
1635 MAY 'Strafford' svy [IR/L 67]
1641 MAY svy & distrbn [IR/G 170]
1855 Newport Union GPV ret [IR/L 149]
1856-57 MAY GPV NLI index (Mfc) [Apply to Staff]

Co MEATH (MEA)
1654-56 MEA civ svy [IR/G 19]
c1659 MEA (*parts*) census [IR/C 3]
1663 Kells valuation (Analecta Hibernica 22) [IR/PER]
c1802 MEA Meath Diocese prot ret (Ir Ancestor 5/2) [IR/PER]
1821 MEA census ext (Smith families) (Dun Laoghaire Gencal Soc J 3/4) [IR/PER]
1854 MEA GPV NLI index (Mfc) [Apply to Staff]; Kells Union GPV ret [IR/L 4]; Oldcastle Union GPV ret [IR/L 5]

Co MONAGHAN (MON)
c1659 MON census [IR/C 3]
1858-60 MON GPV NLI index (Mfc) [Apply to Staff]
1861 MON GPV AIH index (Mfc) [Apply to Staff]; Clones Union (pt) GPV ret [IR/L 155]

Co OFFALY: *see King's Co*

QUEEN'S Co (QU)
c1659 QU census [IR/C 3]
1766 Skirk prot census [IR/L 96]
1850-51 QU GPV NLI index (Mfc) [Apply to Staff]

Co ROSCOMMON (ROS)
1641 ROS svy & distrbn [IR/L 94 or IR/G 169]
c1659 ROS census [IR/C 3]
1857-58 ROS GPV NLI index (Mfc) [Apply to Staff]

Co SLIGO (SL)
c1659 SL census [IR/C 3]
1858 SL GPV NLI index (Mfc) [Apply to Staff]

Co TIPPERARY (TIP)
1654 W & N Baronies civ svy [IR/G 16]
c1659 TIP census [IR/C 3]
1850 TIP GPV AIH index (Mfc) [Apply to Staff]
1851 TIP GPV NLI index (Mfc *in 2 ridings*) [Apply to Staff]
1864-70 Shanrahan & Tullagherton prot rets (Ir Ancestor 16/2) [IR/PER]
1873-80 Clogheen Union prot ret (Ir Ancestor 17/1) [IR/PER]

Co TYRONE (TYR)
1654-56 TYR civ svy [IR/G 17]
1841 TYR OAP claims: census exts index (Mfc) [Apply to Staff]
1851 TYR OAP claims: census exts index (Mfc) [Apply to Staff]

1860   TYR GPV NLI index (Mfc) [Apply to Staff]
1901   TYR census (Mfc) [Apply to Staff]

Co WATERFORD (WAT)
c1659   WAT census [IR/C 3]
1821   Waterford City census ext (Ir Gengst 4/1-2) [IR/PER]
1848-51   WAT GPV NLI index (Mfc) [Apply to Staff]
1850   WAT GPV AIH index (Mfc) [Apply to Staff]
1851   WAT GPV ret (Mfc) [Apply to Staff]

Co WESTMEATH (WES)
c1659   WES census [IR/C 3]
c1803   WES Meath Diocese prot ret (Ir Ancestor 5/2) [IR/PER]
1854   WES GPV NLI index (Mfc) [Apply to Staff]

Co WEXFORD (WEX)
1654-56   WEX civ svy (exc Forth Barony) [IR/G 23]
c1659   WEX census[IR/C 3]
1853   WEX GPV NLI index (Mfc) [Apply to Staff]
1867   Marshallstown census(Ir Gengst 6/5) [IR/PER]

Co WICKLOW (WIC)
1852-53   WIC GPV NLI index (Mfc) [Apply to Staff]

SCOTLAND

ABERDEENSHIRE (AB)

1636   Old Aberdeen cen (SC N&Q 7/1-2) [SC/PER]
1741   Old Meldrum cen (AB & NE SC FHS J 19) [SC/PER]
1771   Pittodrie Estate svy (AB & NE SC FHS N/L 7) [SC/PER]
1801   Peterhead cen [SC/C 9]
1812   Glentannar list (AB & NE SC FHS J 40) [SC/PER]
1851   Aberdeen: St Nicholas cen ext (Shetlanders) (Coontin Kin 3-4) [SC/PER]
1851   **2% Census Sample** [Surname Index Mfc]:
         Aberdeen - lunatic asylum, St Nicholas Poor House & Aberdeen West; Aberdour;
         Clat; Cluny; Insch; Kincardine O'Neil; King Edward; Peterhead; Rayne; Tarves
1861   Fraserburgh cen ext (Highlanders & non-Scots) (AB & NE SC FHS N/L 22)
         [SC/PER]
1881   Aberdeen: St Nicholas cen ext (Shetlanders) (Coontin Kin 8-11) [SC/PER]
1891   Aberdeen cen ext (Shetlanders) (Coontin Kin 16-20) [SC/PER]
1891   SRO Full County Name Index [Mfc]

ANGUS (AN)

1788   Craig cen [Apply to Staff (Shelf 9)]
1851   **2% Census Sample** [Surname Index Mfc]
         Brechin; Crai; Cortachy & Clova; Dundee - Gaol, Royal Infirmary; Inverarity;
         Kirkden; Montrose; Murroes; St Vigeans
1891   SRO Full County Name Index [Mfc]

ARGYLLSHIRE (ARG)

1779 Argyll (Duke of) Estate lists (SC Rec Soc 91) [SC/PER]
1792 Argyll (Duke of) Estate list: Kintyre (SC Rec Soc new ser 17) [SC/PER]
1851 **2% Census Sample** [Surname Index Mfc]
      Cambletown; Canna; Kilarrow; Kilchrenan; Lochgilphead; Morvern; Strachur
1851 Appin [Mf 2506]   Lismore [Mf 2506]
      Ballachulish [Mf 2506]   Lochgilphead [Mf 2506]
      Duror [Mf 2506]   Morvern [Mf 2506]
      Glencoe [Mf 2506]   Muckairn [Mf 2506]

1891 SRO Full County Name Index [Mfc]

AYRSHIRE(AYR)

1841 Galston [Mf 2509]   Kilbirnie [Mf 2509]
      Girvan [Mf 2509]   Kilmarnock [Mf 2509]
      Irvine [Mf 2509]   Kilmaurs [Mf 2509]

1851 **2% Census Sample** [Surname Index Mfc]
      Ardrossen; Colmonel; Dallmellington; Dreghorn; Galston; Girvan; Irvine; Kilbirnie; Kilmarnock; Kilmaurs; Kirkmichael; Loudon; Mauchline; Newton upon Ayre;
1891 SRO Full County Name Index [Mfc]

BANFFSHIRE (BAN)

BAN = Index to Surnames in 1851 Census for Banffshire Vols 1-4 by Margaret Shand
1851 Alvah (BAN 2) [SC/C 5A]   Forglen (BAN 1) [SC/C 5]
      Banff (BAN 3) [SC/C 5B]   Gamrie (BAN 2) [SC/C 5A]
      Boyndie (BAN 3)[SC/C 5B]   Inverkeithny (BAN 1) [SC/C 5]
      Cullen (BAN 4) [SC/C 5C]   Marnoch (BAN1) [SC/C 5]
      Deskford (BAN 4) [SC/C 5C]   Ordiquil (BAN 3) [SC/C 5B]
      Fordyce (BAN4) [SC/C 5C]   Rothiemay (BAN 1) [SC/C 5]

1851 **2% Census Sample** [Surname Index Mfc]
      Belhelvie; Boyndie; Kirkmichael; Rathven; St Fergus
1891 SRO Full County Name Index [Mfc]

BERWICKSHIRE (BER)

1851 All parish returns held
      Abbey St Bethans - Eccles [Mf 3477-3478]
      Edrom - Whitsome & Hilton [Mf 2758]
1851 **2% Census Sample** [Surname Index Mfc]
      Merton; Whitsome & Hilton
1891 SRO Full County Name Index [Mfc]

BUTESHIRE (BUT)

1851 AWS = Argyle & West Scotland Census Index - County complete
      Buteshire (AWS 1) [Mfc]
1851 **2% Census Sample** [Surname Index Mfc]
      Rothsay
1891 SRO Full County Name Index [Mfc]

CAITHNESS (CAT)

1851 Bower [Mf 2414]
Canisbay & Keiss [Mf 2414]
Dunnet [Mf 2414]
Halkirk [Mf 2414]
Wick (landward) [SP 123/1]

1851 **2% Census Sample** [Surname Index Mfc]
Halkirk
1891 SRO Full County Name Index [Mfc]

CLACKMANNANSHIRE (CL)

1851 **2% Census Sample** [Surname Index Mfc]
Clackmannan
1891 SRO Full County Name Index [Mfc]

DUMBARTONSHIRE (DNB)

1851 **2% Census Sample** [Surname Index Mfc]
Bonhilll; Dunbarton barracks; Helensburgh prison; Kirtinloch jail; Strontian
1891 SRO Full County Name Index [Mfc]

DUMFRIESSHIRE (DMF)

1801 Annan cen (SC Rec Soc new ser 4) [SC/PER]
1811 Annan cen (SC Rec Soc new ser 4) [SC/PER]
1821 Annan cen (SC Rec Soc new ser 4) [SC/PER]
1851 Applegarth (& Sibbaldbie) [SC/C2]
Canonbie [SC/C2]
Cummertrees [SC/C2]
Durrisdeer [SC/C2]
Johnstone [Apply to staff (Shelf 9)]
Langholm [Mf 2849]
Lochmaben [Mf 2849]
Middlebie [Mf 2849]
Moffat [Mf 2849]
Morton [Mf 2849]
Mousewald [Mf 2849]
Penpont [Mf 587]
Ruthwell [Mf 587]
Sanquhar [Mf 587]
St Mungo [Mf 587]
Tinwald [Mf 587]
Torthorwald [Mf 587]
Tundergarth [Mf 587]
Tynron [Mf 587]
Wamphray [Mf 587]
Wanlockhead [Mf 587]
Westerkirk [Mf 587]

1851 **2% Census Sample** [Surname Index Mfc]
Cummertrees; Dumfries; Holywood; Sanquhar
1891 SRO Full County Name Index [Mfc]

EAST LOTHIAN OR HADDINGTONSHIRE (EL)

1851 Berwick, North [Mf 3313]
Morham [Mf 3313]
Oldhamstocks [Mf 3313]
Ormiston [Mf 3313]
Pencaitland [Mf 3313]
Prestonkirk [Mf 3313]
Prestonpans [Mf 3313]
Salton [Mf 3313]
Spott [Mf 3313]
Stenton [Mf 3313]

1851 **2% Census Sample** [Surname Index Mfc]
Dunbar; Haddington
1891 SRO Full County Name Index [Mfc]

ELGIN see Moray

FIFE (FIF)

1851 Abbotshall [Mf 584]
Abdie [Mf 584]
Aberdour [Mf 584]
Anstruther - Easter [Mf 584]
Anstruther - Wester [Mf 584]

Arngask [Mf 584]
Auchterderran [Mf 584]
Auchtermuchty [Mf 584]
Auchtermuchty (*index*) [SC/C 7]
Auchtertool [Mf 584]

1851 **2% Census Sample** [Surname Index Mfc]
Abbotshall; Crail; Dalgety; Dunfermline; Kilmany; Markinch
1891 SRO Full County Name Index [Mfc]

FORFARSHIRE: see Angus

HADDINGTON: see East Lothian

INVERNESS (IN)

1851 AWS = Argyle & West Scotland Census Index
Abernethy (AWS 7) [Mfc]
Alvie (AWS 7) [Mfc]
Ardersier (AWS 8) [Mfc]
Boleskine & Abertaff (AWS 8) [Mfc]
Bracadale, Isle of Skye (AWS 3-4) [Mfc]
Croy (AWS 8) [Mfc]
Dalcross (AWS 8) [Mfc]
Dalrossie (AWS 7) [Mfc]
Daviot (AWS 8) [Mfc]
Dores (AWS 8) [Mfc]
Dunlichty (AWS 8) [Mfc]
Duthil (AWS 7) [Mfc]
Fort Augustus (AWS 8) [Mfc]
Glenelg (AWS 9) [Mfc]
Glenmoriston (AWS 9) [Mfc]
Inverness (AWS 2) [Mfc]
Insh *see* Kingussie

Lagan (AWS 7) [Mfc]
Kilmonivaig (AWS 7) [Mfc] & [Mf 2359]
Kilmorack [Mf 2359]
Kilmuir (AWS 8) [Mfc]
Kingussie (AWS 7) [Mfc]
Kiltarlity (AWS9) [Mfc]
Kingussie & Insh (AWS 7) [Mfc]
Kingussie & Insh [Mf 2359]
Kirkhill (AWS 8) [Mfc]
Moy & Dalrossie (AWS 7) [Mfc]
Petty (AWS 8) [Mfc]
Portree (AWS 8?) [Mfc]
Rothiemurchas (AWS 8) [Mfc]
Sleat (AWS 8) [Mfc]
Snizort (AWS 3-4) [Mfc]
Strath (AWS3-4) [Mfc]

1851 **2% Census Sample** [Surname Index Mfc]
Ardnamuchan; Boleskine & Abertaff; Dalrossie; Kilmuir
1891 SRO Full County Name Index [Mfc]

KINCARDINESHIRE (KNC)

1891 SRO Full County Name Index [Mfc]

KINROSSHIRE (KNR)

1891 SRO Full County Name Index [Mfc]

KIRKUDBRIGHTSHIRE (KRK)

1684 Minnigaff list (SC Rec Soc 50) [SC/PER]

1841 Anwoth [Mf 2618]
Balmaclellan [Mf 2618] or [Shelf 9]
Balmaghie [Mf 2618]
Borgue [Mf 2618]

Buittle [Mf 2618]
Carsphairn [Mf 2618]
Colvend [Mf 2618]
Crossmichael [Mf 2618]

1851 Anwoth [Mf 2619]
Balmaclellan [Mf 2619]
Balmaghie [Mf 2618]
Borgue [Mf 2619]
Buittle [Mf 2619]

Carsphairn [Mf 2619]
Colvend [Mf 2619]
Crossmichael [Mf 2619]
Dalry [Mf 2619]

1851 **2% Census Sample** [Surname Index Mfc]
Drumoak; Girthon; Kirkpatrick Durham
1891 SRO Full County Name Index {Mfc]

LANARKSHIRE (LKS)

1851 LKS cen ext (N Scots) (AB & NE SC FHS N/L 26) [SC/PER] & [Mf 2500]
1851 **2% Census Sample** [Surname Index Mfc]
Bothwell; Cadder; Carmichael; Dairy; Douglas; East Kilbride; Glasgow (Barony, Calton, Gorbals, Infantry barracks, North prison, Poor house, St George's, St James, St John's, St Mary, St Mungo's, St Paul's); New Monkland; Shotts
1891 SRO Full County Name Index [Mfc]

MID LOTHIAN (MID)

1841 Fala & Soutra [Mf 2710]
Glencross [Mf 2710]
Heriot [Mf 2710]

Inveresk [Mf 2710]
Kirknewton & East Calder [Mf 2710]
Lasswade [Mf 2710]

1851 EDI = Edinburgh 1851 Census transcription & Index Vol 1 - 3 - N R & S Carstairs
Edinburgh Canongate [Mf 2431] & (EDI 1) [S/C 3]
Edinburgh Castle (EDI 1) [SC/C 4]
Edinburgh Old City (EDI 2) [SC/C 3]
Edinburgh New Town (EDI 3, pts 1 & 2) [SC/C 12]
Edinburgh St Cuthbert [Mf 2431]
Fala and Soutra [Mf 2711]
Glencross [Mf 2711]
Heriot [Mf 2711]
Inveresk [Mf 2711]
Kirknewton and East calder [Mf 2711]
Lasswade [Mf 2711]
1851 **2% Census Sample** [Surname Index]
Crichton; Dalkeith poor house; Edinburgh Canongate; Edinburgh Castle; Edinburgh (City poor house, George Watson Hospital, Old Greyfriars, Old Church, St Cuthbert's charity workhouse, Prison, Royal Infirmary, St George's ,St Mary); Leith
1881 Leith, North & South [Mf 589-581]
1891 SRO Full County Name Index [Mfc]

MORAY (MOR) or ELGIN

1851 **2% Census Sample** [Surname Index Mfc]
Duffas; Forres
1891 SRO Full County Name Index [Mfc]

NAIRNSHIRE (NRN)

1851 2% Census Sample [Surname Index Mfc]
Cawdor; Fort George garrison
1891 SRO Full County Name Index [Mfc]

ORKNEY (ORK)

1851 Walls [Mf 1281]
1851 2% Census Sample [Surname Index Mfc]
Kirkwall; Shapinsay; Westray
1891 SRO Full County Name Index [Mfc]

PEEBLESHIRE (PEB)

1851 2% Census Sample [Surname Index Mfc]
Eddlestone
1891 SRO Full County Name Index [Mfc]

PERTHSHIRE (PER)

1851 2% Census Sample [Surname Index Mfc]
Auchdergaven; Cargill; Dunning; Killin; Kincardine; Kirkmichael; Moulin; Mutchill; Perth (Female school of industry, Murray's asylum for lunatics, St Paul's); St Maddoes
1871 Balquidder [Mf 2430]
Bendochy [Mf 2430]
Blackford [Mf 2430]
Blair-Atholl [Mf 2430]
Blairgowrie [Mf 2430]
Callender [Mf 2430]
Caputh [Mf 2430]
Cargill [Mf 2430]
Clunie [Mf 2430]
Collace [Mf 2430]
Comrie [Mf 2430]
Crieff [Mf 2430]
Culross [Mf 2430]
Strowan [Mf 2430]

1891 SRO Full County Name Index [Mfc]

RENFREWSHIRE (REN)

1841 Erskine [Mf 2847-2848]
Greenock [Mf 2847-2848]
Paisley [Mf 356-357]
1851 Greenock [Mf 1833-1835]
Port Glasgow [Mf 1836]
Paisley [Mf 358-359]
Renfrew *part* [Mf 1836]
1851 2% Census Sample [Surname Index Mfc]
Neilston; Paisley (Abbey, Middle Church)
1861 Paisley [Mf 360]
1891 SRO Full County Name Index [Mfc]

ROSS & CROMARTY (ROS)

1792 Ross-shire list (Highland FHS J 10) [SC/PER]
1841 Ross & Cromarty County Index [SC/C 10]

1841 Dingwall [Mf 1531]
Edderton [Mf 1531]
Fearn [Mf 1531]
Foddety [Mf 1531]
Gairloch [Mf 1531]
Glenshiel [Mf 1531]
Killearnan [Mf 1531]
Kilmuir Easter [Mf 1531]
Kiltearn [Mf 1531]

Kincardine [Mf 2358]
Kintail [Mf 2538]
Knockbain [Mf 2538]
Lochalsh [Mf 2538]
Lochbroom [Mf 2538]
Lochcarron [Mf 2538]
Logie Easter [Mf 2538]
Nigg [Mf 2538]
Poolewe (see Gairloch) [Mf 1531]

1851 AWS = Argyle & West Scotland Census Index
HFS = Highland FHS Census Indexes
Applecross (AWS 5) [Mfc]
Alness (AWS 10) [Mfc]
Contin (AWS 6) [Mfc]
Dingwall [Mf 1884] & (AWS10) [Mfc]
Edderton [Mf 1884] & (AWS 10) [Mfc]
Fearn [Mf 1884] & (AWS 11) [Mfc]
Foderty [Mf 1884] & (AWS 10) [Mfc]
Gairloch [Mf 1884] & (AWS 5) [Mfc]
Glenshiel (AWS 6) [Mfc]
Killearnan (HFS) [SC/C 11]
Kilmuir Easter (AWS 11) [Mfc]
Kiltearn [SP 82/3] & (AWS 10) [Mfc]
Kincardine (with Croik) (AWS 6) [Mfc]

Kincardine (with Croik) (HFS) [SC/C 11]
Kintail (AWS 6) [Mfc]
Knockbain [SP 123/4]
Lochalsh (AWS 6) [Mfc]
Lochbroom (AWS 5) [Mfc]
Lochcarron (AWS 6) [Mfc]
Logie Easter (AWS 11) [Mfc]
Nigg (AWS 11) [Mfc]
Poolewe (see Gairloch) [Mf 1884]
Tain (AWS 11) [Mfc] & (HFS) [SC/C 11]
Tarbat (AWS 11) [Mfc]
Urray (AWS 6) [Mfc]

1851 **2% Census Sample** [Surname Index Mfc]
Contin; Duffas; Forres; Rosskeen

1861 Alness [Mf 1885]
Applecross [Mf 1885]
Avoch [Mf 1885]
Contin [Mf 1885]
Dingwall [Mf 1885]
Edderton [Mf 1885]
Gairloch [Mf 1885]
Glenshiel [Mf 1885]
Killearnan [Mf 2360]

Kiltearn [Mf 2360]
Kincardine [Mf 2360]
Kintail [Mf 2360]
Knockbain [Mf 2360]
Lochalsh [Mf 2360]
Lochbroom [Mf 2360]
Lochcarron [Mf 2360]
Logie Easter [Mf 2360]
Poolewe *see* Gairloch

1871 Edderton [Mf 1886]
Fearn [Mf 1886]
Fodderty [Mf 1886]
Gairloch [Mf 1886]
Glenshiel [Mf 1886]
Logie Easter [Mf 2333]
Logie Wester *see* Urquart
Nigg [Mf 2333]

Poolewe *see* Gairloch
Resolis [Mf 2333]
Roskeen [Mf 2333]
Tain [Mf 2333]
Tarbat [Mf 2333]
Urqhart [Mf 2333]
Urray [Mf 2333]

1881 Dingwall [Mf 1887]
Edderton [Mf 1887]
Fearn [Mf 1887]
1891 SRO Full County Name Index [Mfc]

ROXBURGHSHIRE (ROX)

1851 **2% Census Sample** [Surname Index Mfc]
      Castleton; Calvers; Ednam; Hawick; Hobkirk; Hownam; Jedburgh; Kelso; Robertson

1871 Cavers [Mf 2335A]   Hawick [Mf 2335A]
      Crailing [Mf 2335A]   Hobkirk [Mf 2335A]
      Eckford [Mf 2335A]   Hownam [Mf 2335A]
      Edgerston [Mf 2335A]   Jedburgh [Mf 2335A]
      Ednam [Mf 2335A]

1891 SRO Full County Name Index [Mfc]

SELKIRKSHIRE (SEL)

1891 SRO Full County Name Index [Mfc]

SHETLAND (SH)

1785, 1829, 1841, 1845 Fair Isle [SC/L 88]

1851 Aithsting [Mf 1280]   Papa Stour [Mf 1281]
      Bressay [Mf 1279]   Quarff [Mf 1279]
      Burra [Mf 1279]   Sandness [Mf 1281]
      Cinningsburgh [Mf 1279]   Sandsting [Mf 1279]
      Delting [Mf 1279]   Sandwick [Mf 1279]
      Dunrossness [Mf 1279]   Skerries (see Whalsey) [Mf 1280]
      Fair Isle [Mf 1279] & [SC/L 88] Tingwall [Mf 1281]
      Fetlar [Mf 1279]   Unst [Mf 1281]
      Foula [Mf 1281]   Whalsay & Skerries [Mf 1280]
      Lerwick [Mf 1280]   Whiteness & Weesdale [Mf 1281]
      Lunnasting [Mf 1280]   Yell, Mid [Mf 1280]
      Nesting [Mf 1280]   Yell, North [Mf 1279]
      Northmavine [Mf 1280]   Yell, South [Mf 1280]

1851 **2% Census Sample** [Surname Index Mfc]
      Delting; Tingwall
1861 Fair Isle [SC/L 88]
1871 Shipping cen (ZET strays) (Coontin Kin 3-5) [SC/PER]
1891 SRO Full County Name Index [Mfc]

STIRLINGSHIRE (ST)

1851 Falkirk [Mf 1390]
1851 **2% Census Sample** [Surname Index Mfc]
      Falkirk; Kilsyth; Larbert; Muiravonside; Stirling
1891 SRO Full County Name Index [Mfc]

SUTHERLAND (SUT)

1841 Asynt [Mf 2357] or [Mf 2454]   Durness [Mf 2357] or [Mf 2454]
      Clyne [Mf 2357] or [Mf 2454]   Eddrachillis [Mf 2357] or [Mf 2454]
      Creich [Mf 2357] or [Mf 2454]   Farr [Mf 2357] or [Mf 2454]
      Dornoch [Mf 2357] or [Mf 2454] Golspie [Mf 2357] or [Mf 2454]

Kildonan [Mf 2357] or [Mf 2454] Rogart [Mf 2357] or [Mf 2454]
Lairg [Mf 2357] or [Mf 2454] Tongue [Mf 2357] or [Mf 2454]
Loth [Mf 2357] or [Mf 2454]

1851 Aassynt [Mf 2373] Dornoch [Mf 2373]
Clyne [Mf 2373] Durness [Mf 2373]
Creich [Mf 2373]

1851 **2% Census Sample** [Surname Index Mfc]
Farr; Tonge

1861 Assynt [Mf 2628] Golspie [Mf 2628]
Clyne [Mf 2628] Kildonan [Mf 2628]
Creich [Mf 2628] Lairg [Mf 2628]
Dornoch [Mf 2628] Loth [Mf 2628]
Durness [Mf 2628] Rogart [Mf 2628]
Eddrachillis [Mf 2628] Tongue [Mf 2628]
Farr [Mf 2628]

1871 Farr [Mf 2332] Loth [Mf 2332]
Golspie [Mf 2332] Rogart [Mf 2332]
Kildonan [Mf 2332] Tongue [Mf 2332]
Lairg [Mf 2332]

1891 SRO Full County Name Index [Mfc]

WEST LOTHIAN (WL)

1891 Full County Name Index [Mfc]

WIGTOWNSHIRE (WIG)

1684 WIG parish lists (SC Rec Soc 50) [SC/PER]
1832 Portpatrick 'Urquhart' cen (SC Rec Soc new ser 8) [SC/PER]
1844 Portpatrick 'Urquhart' cen (SC Rec Soc new ser 8) [SC/PER]
1846 Portpatrick 'Urquhart' cen (SC Rec Soc new ser 8) [SC/PER]
1852 Portpatrick 'Urquhart' cen (SC Rec Soc new ser 8) [SC/PER]
1851 **2% Census Sample** [Surname Index Mfc]
Kirkcolm; Old Luce; Sorbie
1891 SRO Full County Name Index [Mfc]

WALES

ANGLESEY (AGY)
1767 AGY papist return (CRS Occ Paper 2) [RC/PER]

ANGLESEY **1851**
GFH = Gwynedd FHS 1851 census Indexes   * = Microfilm held
REGISTRATION DISTRICT	HO 107	Volume	Location
Angelsey RD	2520-2522*	GFH 21	Mfc
Bangor RD - Angelsey *part*	2517-2518*	GFH 21	Mfc
Carnarvon RD			

- Angelsey *part* 2515-2516* GFH 21 Mfc
- Landwrog SD[ff1-120,520-end] 2515* GFH 21 Mfc
- Llandichen SD [340-end] 2516*

ANGLESEY **1861**
REGISTRATION DISTRICT RG 9
Angelsey RD 4361-4371*

ANGLESEY **1881**
GSU Transcript & Indexes - county complete [Lower Library Mfc]

BRECKNOCKSHIRE (BRE)
1767   BRE papist return (CRS Occ Paper 2) [RC/PER]

BRECKNOCKSHIRE **1841-1881**
Ystra Wy [WS/C 14]

BRECKNOCKSHIRE **1851**
REGISTRATION DISTRICT HO 107
Brecknock RD 2489
Builth RD 2488
Crickhowell RD 2490
Hay RD 2491
Llandovery RD - Brecknockshire part 2470*
Merthyr Tydvil RD - Brecknockshire part 2457-2460*
Rhayarder RD - Brecknockshire part 2494*

BRECKNOCKSHIRE **1881**
GSU Transcript & Indexes - county complete [Lower Library Mfc]

CARDIGANSHIRE (CGN)
1767   CGN papist return (CRS Occ Paper 2) [RC/PER]

CARDIGANSHIRE **1851**
Dyffed FHS 1851 Census Transcripts & Indexes of Major Towns [WDF]
REGISTRATION DISTRICT HO 107 Volume Location
Aberayon RD 2484*
Aberystwyth RD 2485-2586*
Cardigan RD 2481*
 - Cardigan SD (St Dogmaels & St
   Mary) inc Bridge End Hamlet 2481*[ff322-512] WDF 5   WS/C 5 & 6
Lampeter RD 2483*
Newcastle in Emlyn RD 2482*
Tregaron RD 2487*

CARDIGANSHIRE **1861**
REGISTRATION DISTRICT RG 9   REGISTRATION DISTRICT RG 9
Aberayon RD 4190-4193*   Lampeter RD 4186-4189*
Aberystwyth RD 4194-4200*   Newcastle in Emlyn RD 4179-4189*
Cardingan RD 4173-4178*   Tregaron RD 4201-4204*

CARDIGANSHIRE **1881**
GSU Transcript & Indexes - county complete [Lower Library Mfc]

CARMARTHENSHIRE (CMN)

CARMARTHENSHIRE 1851
Dyffed FHS 1851 Census Transcripts & Indexes of Major Towns [WDF]
REGISTRATION DISTRICT	HO 107	Volume	Location
Carmarthen RD	2427-2474*		
- Carmarthen SD	2473 [ff 19-373]	WDF 2	WS/C 1 & 6
Llandilofawr RD	2471*		
Llandovery RD	2470*		
Llanelli RD	2468-2469*		
- Llanelli SD	2468*[ff 124-464]	WDF 1	WS/C 1 & 6

CARMARTHENSHIRE 1861
REGISTRATION DISTRICT	RG 9
Carmarthen RD	4134-4145*
Llandilofawr RD	4127-4133*
Llandovery RD	4118-4126*
Llanelli RD	2468-2469*

CARMARTHENSHIRE 1881
GSU Transcript & Indexes - county complete [Lower Library Mfc]

CAERNARVONSHIRE (CAE)

1767   CAE papist retURN (CRS Occ Paper 2) [RC/PER]

CARNARVONSHIRE 1851
GFH = Gwynedd FHS Census Indexes
REGISTRATION DISTRICT	HO 107	Volume	Location
Bangor RD	2517-1518*		
- Beaumaris SD	2517*	GFH 21	Mfc
- Bangor & Llanllechid SDs	2518*[ff1-689 end]	GFH 3,25, 27-29	Mfc
Carnarvon RD	2515-2516*		
- Llanring SD [ff 222-519]	2515*	GFH 33-34	Mfc
- Carnarvon SD [ff1-339]	2515*	GFH 12, 24	Mfc
Conway RD	2519*		
- Conway SD [ff 5-104]	2519*	GFH 3, 2	Mfc
- Creuddyn SD [ff 182-226,292-304]	2519*	GFH 10-11	Mfc
- Llechwed-lasf SD [ff338-416 end]	2519*	GFH 11	Mfc
Pwllheli RD	2513-2514*		
- Criccieth SD *part*	2513*	GFH 18,17,13	Mfc
- Pwllheli SD *part* [215-310]	2513*	GFH 14-16	Mfc
- Aberdaron SD [ff 125-138]	2514*	GFH 19	Mfc
- Nevin SD *part*	2514*	GFH 20,26,23	Mfc
Llanrwst RD - Carnarvonshire part	2508*		

CARNARVONSHIRE 1861
GFH = Gwynned FHS Census Indexes
REGISTRATION DISTRICT	RG 9	Volume	Location
Bangor RD	4346-3456*		
Carnarvon RD	4336-4345*		

Conway RD 4357-4360*
- Llandudno parish 4358* GFH 5 Mfc
Pwllheli RD 4328-4335*

CARNARVONSHIRE 1881
GSU Transcript & Indexes - county complete [Lower Library Mfc]

DENBIGHSHIRE (DEN)
1767   DEN papist return (CRS Occ Paper 2) [RC/PER]

DENBIGHSHIRE 1841
HUNDRED   HO 107
Isdulas & Ruthvin   1403-1404*

DENBIGHSHIRE 1851
REGISTRATION DISTRICT   HO 107
Llanrwst RD   2508*
Ruthin RD   2504-2505*
St Asaph RD   2506-2507*
Wrexham RD   2502-2503*
Conway RD - Denbighshire part 2519*
Corwen RD - Denbighshire part 2509*

DENBIGHSHIRE 1861
REGISTRATION DISTRICT   RG 9
Llanrwst RD   4304-4307*
Ruthin RD   4289-4294*
St Asaph RD   4295-4302*
Wrexham RD   4277-4288*

DENBIGHSHIRE 1881
GSU Transcript & Indexes - county complete [Lower Library Mfc]

FLINTSHIRE (FLN)
1767   FLN papist return (*in 2 vols*) (CRS Occ Papers 1 & 2) [RC/PER]

FLINTSHIRE 1851
REGISTRATION DISTRICT   HO 107
Holywell RD   2500-2501*
Gt Boughton RD - Flintshire part 2171-2172*
St Asaph RD - Flintshire part 2506-2507*
Wrexham RD - Flintshire part 2502-2503*

FLINTSHIRE 1861
REGISTRATION DISTRICT   RG 9
Holywell RD   4273-4276*

FLINTSHIRE 1881
GSU Transcript & Indexes - county complete [Lower Library Mfc]

GLAMORGANSHIRE (GLA)
1767 GLA papist ret (CRS Occ Paper 2) [RC/PER]

GLAMORGAN 1841
The 1841 districts were based upon the Hundreds.
Glamorgan FHS 1841 Census Transcripts & Index [WGF].   * = Microfilm held

DISTRICT/HUNDRED	HO 107	Volume	Location
Gower	1424	WGF	Mfc
Merthyr Tydfil	1414-1415	WGF	Mfc
Miskin	1420*		
Neath	1421*		
Newcastle & Ogmore	1422-1423*		
Swansea & Cardiff	1424-1426*		

GLAMORGAN 1851
Glamorgan FHS 1851 Census Transcripts & Index [WGF] - County complete

REGISTRATION DISTRICT	HO 107	Volume	Location
Brigend RD - Brigend SD	2461	WGF	Mfc
Cardiff RD			
- Caerphily SD	2454*	WGF	Mfc
- Cardiff SD	2455*	WGF	Mfc
- Llantrissant SD	2456*	WGF	Mfc
Merthyr Tydfil RD			
- Gelligaer SD	2457*	WGF	Mfc
- Merthyr Tydfil Lower SD	2458*	WGF	Mfc
- Merthyr Tydfil Upper SD	2459*	WGF	Mfc
- Aberdare SD	2460*	WGF	Mfc
Neath RD			
- Margam SD	2462*	WGF	Mfc
- Neath SD	2463*	WGF	Mfc
- Cadoxton SD	2464*	WGF	Mfc
Swansea RD			
- Llangyfellach SD	2465*	WGF	Mfc
- Swansea SD	2466*	WGF	Mfc
- Gower SD	2467*	WGF	Mfc
Llanelli RD - Glamorgan part	2468-2469*		
Newport RD - Glamorgan part	2451-2453*		

GLAMORGAN 1861

REGISTRATION DISTRICT	RG 9	REGISTRATION DISTRICT	RG 9
Brigend RD	4072-4079*	Merthyr Tydfil RD	4045-4071*
Cardiff RD	4028-4044*	Neath RD	4080-4090*
Gower RD	4108-4109*	Swansea RD	4095-4107*

GLAMORGAN 1881
GSU Transcript & Indexes - county complete [Lower Library Mfc]

Glamorgan FHS 1881 Census Transcripts & Index [WGF]

REGISTRATION DISTRICT	RG 11	Volume	Location
Gower & Llanelli RD *part*	5367-5370	WGF	Mfc

GLAMORGAN **1891**
Glamorgan FHS 1891 Census Transcripts & Index [WGF]
REGISTRATION DISTRICT RG 12 Volume Location
Neath RD - Margam SD 4457-4459 WGF Mfc

MERIONETHSHIRE (MER)
1767 MER papist ret (CRS Occ Paper 2) [RC/PER]

MERIONETHSHIRE **1841**
THe 1841 districts were based upon the Hundreds. The Society hold the following films:
DISTRICT/HUNDRED HO 107
Ardudwy & Edernion 1427-1428
Estimaner & Penllyn 1429-1430
Talybont/Mowddwy/Dolgelly 1431-1432

MERIONETHSHIRE **1851**
REGISTRATION DISTRICT HO 107 REGISTRATION DISTRICT HO 107
Bala RD 2510* Dolgelly RD 2511*
Corwen RD 2509* Festiniog RD 2512

MERIONETHSHIRE **1861**
REGISTRATION DISTRICT RG 9 REGISTRATION DISTRICT RG 9
Bala RD 4314-4316* Dolgelly RD 4317-4321*
Corwen RD 4308-4313* Festiniog RD 4322-4327*

MERIONETHSHIRE **1881**
GSU Transcript & Indexes - county complete [Lower Library Mfc]

MONMOUTHSHIRE (MON)

MONMOUTHSHIRE **1851**
REGISTRATION DISTRICT HO 107 REGISTRATION DISTRICT HO 107
Abergavenny RD 2446-2448* Newport RD 2451-2453*
Chepstow RD 2443* Pontypool RD 2449-2450*
Monmouth RD 2444-2445

MONMOUTHSHIRE **1861**
REGISTRATION DISTRICT RG 9 REGISTRATION DISTRICT RG 9
Abergavenny RD 3991-3996* Monmouth RD 3980-3990*
Bedwelty RD 3997-4006* Newport RD 4013-4027*
Chepstow RD 3974-3979* Pontypool RD 4007-4012*

MONMOUTHSHIRE **1881**
GSU Transcript & Indexes - county complete [Lower Library Mfc]

MONTGOMERYSHIRE (MGY)
1767 MGY papist return (CRS Occ Paper 2) [RC/PER]

MONTGOMERYSHIRE 1841
The 1841 districts were based on the Hundreds. The Society holds the following films:
DISTRICT/HUNDRED	HO 107
Llanidloes & Mchynllech	1436-1437
Newtown	1440

MONTGOMERYSHIRE 1851
Powys FHS Census Indexes [PFH]
REGISTRATION DISTRICT	HO 107	Volume	Location
Llanfyllin RD	2499	PFH	Mfc
Machynlleth RD	2495		
Montgomery RD	2498		
Newtown RD	2496-2497		
Atcham RD - Montgomery part	1990-1991*		
Clun RD - Montgomery part	1983*		
Dolgelly RD - Montgomery part	2511*		
Oswestry RD - Montgomery part	1993*		

MONTGOMERYSHIRE 1881
GSU Transcripts & Indexes - county complete [Lower Library Mfc]

PEMBROKESHIRE (PEM)
1767   PEM papist return (CRS Occ Paper 2) [RC/PER]

PEMBROKESHIRE 1841
The 1841 districts were based upon the Hundreds. The Society holds the following films:
DISTRICT/HUNDRED	HO 107
Dewisland	1444
Dungleddy	1445
Kemess	1446
Kilgenan & Narberth	1447-1448

PEMBROKESHIRE 1851
Dyffed FHS 1851 Census Transcripts & Indexes of Major Towns [WDF]
REGISTRATION DISTRICT	HO 107	Volume	Location
Haverfordwest RD	2477-2480*		
- Haverfordwest SD [Haroldston St Issells, St Thomas, Portfield (ex par), St Mary, St Martin, Prendergast, Uzmaston]	2478*[ff4-286]	WDF 4	WS/C 4 & 6
Narberth RD	2475*		
Pembroke RD	2476*		
- Pembroke Dock/Pembroke St Mary	2476*[ff322-573]	WDF 3	WS/C 3 & 6
Cardigan RD - Pembroke part	2481*		
Newcastle in Emlyn RD - Pembroke part	2482*		

PEMBROKESHIRE 1861
REGISTRATION DISTRICT	RG 9
Haverfordwest RD	4160-4170*
Narberth RD	4146-4151*
Pembroke RD	4152-4159*

PEMBROKESHIRE 1881
GSU Transcript & Indexes - county complete [Lower Library Mfc]

RADNORSHIRE (RAD)
1767 RAD papist return (CRS Occ Paper 2) [RC/PER]

RADNORSHIRE 1851
REGISTRATION DISTRICT	HO 107
Knighton RD	2493*
Presteigne RD	2492*
Rhayader RD	2494*

Powys FHS 1851 census index - arranged by Hundreds (HD) [PFH]

HUNDRED	DISTRICT	HO 107	Volume	Location
Rhayader HD part Llanfanffraid Cwmteuddwr, Rhayader, St Harmon	Rhayader RD part	2494	PFH 1	WS/C 13
Rhayader HD part Llanfihangel Helysen Llanre, Nantmel	Rhayader RD part	2494	PFH 2	WS/C 13
Knighton HD part - Abbey Cwmhier, Llanbister, Llandwi Ystradenni	Knighton RD part and Rhayader RD part	2493 2494	PFH3	WS/C 13
Knighton HD part Beguildey, Llananno Llanbadarn Fynudd	Knighton RD part and Rhayader RD part	2493 2494	PFH 4	WS/C 13
Knighton HD part Heyhope, Knighton, Stanage	Knighton RD part	2493	PFH 5	WS/C 13
Cefnyllys HD part - Ceffnllys, Llabadarn Fawr, Llandrinod	Rhayader RD part and Builth RD part	2494	PFH 6	WS/C 13
Cefnyllys HD part Bleddfa, Llandegley, Llnafihangel, Rhydithen	Presteigne RD part Knighton RD	2492 2493	PFH 7	WS/C 13
Cefnyllys HD part Llangynllo, Pileton, Whitton	Presteigne RD part	2492	PFH 8	WS/C 13
Radnor HD part Cascob, Radnor Old & New	Presteigne RD part	2492	PFH 9	WS/C 13
Radnor HD part Disgoed, Norton, Presteyne	Presteigne RD part	2492	PFH 10	WS/C 13
Radnor HD part Coffa, Gladestry, Llanfihangel Nant, Melan	Presteigne RD part	2492	PFH 11	WS/C 13

RADNORSHIRE 1881
GSU Transcript & Indexes - county complete [Lower Library Mfc]

OVERSEAS

ATLANTIC ISLANDS (AI)

1833   Falkland Is return [AI/L 5 or L 6]
1841-42   Falkland Is returns [AI/L 5 or L 6]
1851   Falkland Is census [AI/L 5 or L 6]

AUSTRALIA (AUA)

Note: *few censuses have survived for Australia but the Library holds a few substitute records as shown below*

Australian Capital Territory (ACT)
pre-1911   ACT: see New South Wales

New South Wales (NSW)
1800   NSW muster ext (omissions A-K) (Illawarra Branches 33) [AUA/NSW/PER]
1800-02 NSW & Norfolk Is musters [AUA/NSW/G 3]
1805   Norfolk Is muster [AUA/NSW/L 1]
1805-06 NSW & Norfolk Is musters [AUA/NSW/G 17]
1811   NSW & Norfolk Is musters [AUA/NSW/G 5]
1814   NSW muster [AUA/NSW/G 6]
1822   NSW muster [AUA/NSW/G 2]
1828   NSW census [AUA/NSW/C 1 or ext (A-BAT) AUA/NSW/C 2]; NSW pedigrees (A-T) (AUAn Gengst 1/2-2/9, 2/11, 3/1, 3/3-4/7, 4/9) [AUA/PER]; NSW census ext (Illawarra omissions) (Illawarra Branches 24) [AUA/NSW/PER]
1837   NSW convict ret [AUA/NSW/G 4 or AUA/NSW/G 18 or ext (name changes) (Illawarra Branches 25) [AUA/NSW/PER]; Canberra convict ret (Ancestral Searcher 5/4) [AUA/ACT/PER]; Illawarra & the S Coast convict ret (Illawarra Branches 16-22) [AUA/NSW/PER]
1841   Illawarra census ext (K only) (Illawarra Branches 23) [AUA/NSW/PER]

Northern Territory (NT)
pre-1863   NT: see New South Wales

Queensland (QL)
pre-1859   QL: see New South Wales

Tasmania (T)
1804   Hobart muster ext (non-convicts) (Generation 18/3) [AUA/QL/PER]
1811   Van Dieman's Land muster [AUA/NSW/G 5]
1818   Van Dieman's Land muster [AUA/NSW/L 1]

Victoria (V)
pre-1851 V: see New South Wales
1857   V stock assessment (Mfc) [Lower Library]

Western Australia (WA)
1832   WA census [AUA/WA/C 1]

CANADA (CAN)

Dominion-wide
1667 CAN census ext (important families) (New Orleans Genesis 7/28) [US/LA/PER]

British Columbia (BC)
1901 Kamloops census ext (Provincial Home) (Family Footsteps 11/1) [CAN/BC/PER]

Manitoba (MA)
1875 New Iceland list (Generations 4/1) [CAN/MA/PER]

Newfoundland & Labrador (NL)
1789 St John's convict ret ext (Irish born) (Dun Laoghaire Gencal Soc J 1/4) [IR/PER]
1794 Petty Harbour census (NL Ancestor 8/2) [CAN/NL/PER]
1836 Fogo census (NL Ancestor 6/3); River Head, Harbour Grace list (NL Ancestor 5/3) [*both* CAN/NL/PER]
1849 Humber Arm, Bay of Is list (NL Gencal Soc N/L 3/2) [CAN/NL/PER]

Nova Scotia (NS)
1752 Cape Breton Is census ext (NL born) (NL Ancestor 6/3) [CAN/NL/PER]
1770 NS census [CAN/NS/C 1]; Pictou with Donegal ret [CAN/NS/L 6]
1773 Yarmouth census [CAN/NS/C 1]
1775 Pictou with Donegal ret [CAN/NS/L 6]; St John's River Harbour census [CAN/NS/C 1]
1783 Halifax provisions list (NS Gengst 5/2) [CAN/NS/PER]
1784 Annapolis Co negroes ret (NS Gengst 1/1); Guysborough loyalists list (NS Gengst 1/2) [*both* CAN/NS/PER]
1786 Shelburne Co census ext (Port Roseway associates) (NEHGR 117/1) [US/NE/PER]
1787 Queen's Co census [CAN/NS/C 1]
1790 Little Harbour & Merigomish rets [CAN/NS/L 6]
1809 Merigomish ret [CAN/NS/L 6]
1817 St Margaret's Bay census (NS Gengst 8/3) [CAN/NS/PER]
1818-29 St Mary's Bay families [CAN/NS/L 4]
1820 Halifax: Ship Harbour list (NS Gengst 9/2) [CAN/NS/PER]
1838 Cumberland Co census (NS Gengst 8/2) [CAN/NS/PER]
1840-44 St Mary's Bay families [CAN/NS/L 5]
1866 Yarmouth Co census indian schedule (NS Gengst 10/2) [CAN/NS/PER]

Ontario (ON)
1783-86 ON rets & provisioning lists [CAN/ON/G 8]
1785 Kingston: Cataraqui list (ON Gencal Soc Kingston Branch N/L 4/1) [CAN/ON/PER]
1797 York & dist census (Toronto Tree 24/6) [CAN/ON/PER]
1825 McNab Township lists (SC Gengst 28/3) [SC/PER]
1852 Fitzroy census ext (Tyrone born) (N Ir Roots 5/2) [IR/PER]
1861 Bedford Township census (ON Gencal Soc Kingston Branch N/L 9/5/1) [CAN/ON/PER]; E Gwillimburg & Holland Landing cens (NGSQ 43/4) [US/PER]
1871 ON census (*vols 1-30*) [CAN/ON/C 1-6 & corrections (Newsleaf 24/1) CAN/ON/PER]; ON census ext (NL born) (NL Ancestor 12/2) [CAN/NL/PER]; ON census ext (Nova Scotians) (NS Gengst 6/3) [CAN/NS/PER]; E Gwillimburg & Holland Landing census exts (NGSQ 43/4) [US/PER]
1891 Sudbury census (*surnames*) (Newsleaf 25/1) [CAN/ON/PER]

Quebec (QB)
1825 Shipton [CAN/QB/C 1]
1847 Quebec Town: a parish cadastre (Memoires 8/1, 8/3 & 9/3-4) [CAN/QB/PER]

DENMARK (DEN)

1787 Kundby Sogn (Danish Gencal Helper 1/2); Østerlarsker (Danish Gencal Helper 1/3); Tolne Parish (Danish Gencal Helper 1/1); Tullebølle Sogn (Danish Gencal Helper 1/4); Vissenbjerg (Danish Gencal Helper 1/4) [*all* DEN/PER]
1801 Tullebølle Sogn (Danish Gencal Helper 1/4) [DEN/PER]

FRANCE (FRA)

1756 Bordeaux census ext (Irish born) (Ir Gengst 4/6) [IR/PER]

NEW ZEALAND (NZ)

Note: *apart from a few isolated exceptions no census before 1966 has survived and there appears to be no ideal substitute, but shipping lists and the following may help*

pre-1861 Otago settlers (Mfc) [Apply to Staff]
1863 North Is native land ret (*surnames only*) (NZ Gengst 22/212 & 23/214) [NZ/PER]
1882 Freeholders' ret (Mfc) [Apply to Staff]

SPAIN (SPA)

1709-73 Cadiz census exts (Irish born) (Ir Gengst 6/6) [IR/PER]

UNITED STATES (US)

Note: *Federal Censuses are held every 10 years from 1790 but some remote states did not complete the enumeration until the following year; all other censuses are either State or local Censuses*

States-Wide
1790 US census ext (most frequent surnames) (BIJ 1/1) [US/CA/PER]
1790-1900 US census exts (duplicates) (Am Gengst 54/2, 59/2, 62/2-4) [US/PER]
1800-80 US census exts [US/G 28]

Alabama (AL)
c1780 AL census ext (English born) (NGSQ 70/4) [US/PER]
1830-80 AL census exts [US/G 28]
1850 St Clair Co census ext (missing households) (NGSQ 77/1) [US/PER]

Arkansas (AR)
1850-80 AR census exts [US/G 28]

Arizona (AZ)
1766 Tucson census ext (native Americans) (Copper State Bull 24/3) [US/AZ/PER]

1801   Tucson census ext (native Americans) (Copper State Bull 24/3) [US/AZ/PER]
1831   Santa Cruz census (Copper State Bull 17/2-4); Tubac census (Copper State Bull 17/1); Tucson census (Copper State Bull 16/1-2) [*all* US/AZ/PER]
1880   Bumble Bee census (Copper State Bull 25/4); Peck Mine (*now Alexandra*) census (Copper State Bull 25/3) [*both* US/AZ/PER]
1890   Cochise Co census (Copper State Bull 15/4-17/4) [US/AZ/PER]
1900   AZ census ext (blacks) (Copper State Bull 21/3-4) [US/AZ/PER]

California (CA)
1790   Los Angeles padron ext (Searcher 4/6-7); San Diego presidio padron (Orange Co CGSQ 10/1) [*both* US/CA/PER]
1836   Los Angeles Co census ext (Orange Co CGSQ 15/3) [US/CA/PER]
1850   CA census ext (ME born) (NEHGR 91/3-4) [US/NE/PER]; CA census ext (Nova Scotia born) (NS Gengst 6/1) [CAN/NS/PER]; Los Angeles Co census ext (Orange dist) (Orange Co CGSQ 13/4) [US/CA/PER]; Napa Co census (Napa Val Q 3/2) [US/CA/PER]
1852   CA census ext (surveyors) (Orange Co CGSQ 21/4); Calaveras Co census (Orange Co CGSQ 18/4, 19/2-3 & 20/1 & *ext:* Mother Lode 8/2) [*both* US/CA/PER]
1856   CA census ext (IA men) (Am Gengst 53/1) [US/PER]; CA census ext (MI men) (Detroit Soc Gencal Res Mag 38/4) [US/MI/PER]; CA census ext (NY born) (NY Record 106/2-3) [US/NY/PER]; CA census ext (PA born) (PA Gencal Mag 28/33) [US/PA/PER]; CA census ext (RI men) (Am Gengst 51/4) [US/PER]
1860   Santa Ana (*with Anaheim*) census (Orange Co CGSQ 7/4-8/2) [US/CA/PER]
1870   Santa Ana (*with Anaheim*) census (Orange Co CGSQ 8/3-10/1 or ext (people born outside CA) (Orange Co CGSQ 6/3) [*both* US/CA/PER]
1873-1900   Tuolumne Co great reg exts 1873, 1879, 1890, 1896 & 1900 (Mother Lode 1/3, 3/2, 4/2, 6/1-2, 8/4-9/1, 10/1, 12/1 & 3, 13/1-14/2 & 15/2) [US/CA/PER]
1880   Tuolumne Co census ext (Indians) (Mother Lode 7/1) [US/CA/PER]
1890   Tuolumne Co census ext (Indians) (Mother Lode 7/1) [US/CA/PER]
1904   Elsinore precinct reg (Orange Co CGSQ 24/3) [US/CA/PER]
1916   Santa Barbara Co - Montecito No 1 precinct reg 1916 (Ancestors W 16/3) [US/CA/PER]
1900   Tuolumne Co census (Mother Lode 1/1-2/3, 3/3-4, 4/2-5/2, 6/1-2, 8/2-9/3, 10/1-4); Tuolumne Co great reg ext (Mother Lode 1/3, 3/2, 4/2, 6/1-2, 8/4-9/1, 10/1 & 3, 13/1-14/2 & 15/2) [*both* US/CA/PER]
1906-12   Tuolumne Co 1906, 1908, 1910 & 1912 precinct reg exts (Mother Lode 2/2-3, 3/4, 4/2, 4/4, 9/3, 11/2-4, 12/2-3, 13/1-3 & 14/3) [US/CA/PER]

Colorado (CO)
1860   KS Terr census ext (TN, VA, NC & SC born) [US/KS/C 1]; Georgetown census ext (Griffith mining dist) (CO Gengst 49/3) [US/CO/PER]
1885   Arapahoe Co census (Manufactures Schedules) (CO Gengst 57/1-3) [US/CO/PER]

Connecticut (CT)
1733   Norwalk: Wilton Parish census (NY Record 70/2) [US/NY/PER]
1745   Norwalk: Wilton Parish census (NY Record 70/2) [US/NY/PER]
1790   CT census [US/CT/C 1 & errata (NEHGR 77/1) [US/NE/PER]

Delaware (DE)
1688   Kent Co census (PA Gencal Mag 37/2) [US/PA/PER]
1693   New Sweden Colony census (Gencal Mag NJ 13/53) [US/NJ/PER]
1790   DE census (NGSQ 36/3-38/3, 39/1-41/4 - *pages 57-64 missing*) [US/PER]

District of Columbia (DC): *see Maryland*

Florida (FL)
1786   St Augustine census ext (Scots) (SC Gengst 15/3) [SC/PER]
1820-60 FL census exts [US/G 28]
1850   FL census ext (ME, NH, VT, MA, RI & CT born) (NEHGR 76/1) [US/NE/PER];
         Gadsden Co census ext (GA born) (FL Gengst 1/3) [US/FL/PER]

Georgia (GA)
1820   Columbia Co census ext (NGSQ 59/2) [US/PER]
1820-70 GA census exts [US/G 28]

Idaho (ID)
1850   OR Terr census [US Tracts]

Illinois (IL)
1850   Calhoun Co census ext (Buried Treasures 17/3) [US/FL/PER]; Edgar Co census ext (VA/WV born) (NGSQ 36/3, 38/1, 38/3) [US/PER]; Jersey Co census ext (Buried Treasures 16/3) [US/FL/PER]; Lake Co census [US/IL/C 1]; Lawrence Co census ext (Buried Treasures 17/1) [US/FL/PER]
1860   Macoupin Co census ext (NY born) (NY Record 117/2) [US/NY/PER]

Indiana (IN)
1820   Wayne Co census ext (A-HIA) (IN Gengst 1/1-2) [US/IN/PER]

Iowa (IA)
1844   Keokuk Co, IA Terr census (Am Gengst 42/3) [US/PER]
1846   Louisa Co census (Am Gengst 43/2) [US/PER]
1847   Clinton Co cen (Am Gengst 43/1); Davis Co cen (Am Gengst 42/4) [*both* US/PER]
1870   IA census ext [US/G 28]

Kansas (KS)
1855   KS census ext (Wyandot Indians) (KS City Gengst 28/1-2) [US/MO/PER]
1860   KS Terr census ext (TN, VA, NC & SC born) [US/KS/C 1]
1880   Wichita Co census (Ancestors W 18/1) [US/CA/PER]

Kentucky (KY)
1820-50 KY census exts [US/G 28]
1842   Frankfort census ext (free blacks) (NGSQ 63/4) [US/PER]
1870   Boyd Co census ext (White Creek WV dist) (Kyowva Gencal Soc N/L 17/1-2) [US/PER]
1880   KY census ext (Buried Treasures 18/2) [US/FL/PER]
1900   KY census ext (Buried Treasures 18/2) [US/FL/PER]

Louisiana (LA)
1731   New Orleans: d'Artaguette census (New Orleans Genesis 5/20-21 -*incomplete*) [US/LA/PER]
1749   New Orleans: German Coast census (New Orleans Genesis 7/26) [US/LA/PER]
1766   New Orleans: German Coast census (New Orleans Genesis 7/25); St Charles Parish census (New Orleans Genesis 7/25) [*both* US/LA/PER]
1792   Opelousas census ext (free blacks & mulattos) (LA Gencal Reg 39/2) [US/LA/PER]
1796   New Orleans census ext (slave masters) (LA Gencal Reg 40/3) [US/LA/PER]
1800   Catahoula Lake census (LA Gencal Reg 39/4); Cotile census (LA Gencal Reg 39/4); Rapides dist census (LA Gencal Reg 39/4) [*all* US/LA/PER]
1805-09 Attakapas dist census exts (non-Acadians) (LA Gencal Reg 21/1) [US/LA/PER]
1812   St Martin Parish census ext (slave owners) (LA Gencal Reg 21/2-3) [US/LA/PER]

1820-80 LA census exts [US/G 28]
1830 Claiborne Parish census (LA Gencal Reg 19/1) [US/LA/PER]
1850 Livingston Parish census (LA Gencal Reg 22/1) [US/LA/PER]

Maine (ME)
1790 ME census [US/ME/C 8]; ME families (*vols 1-3*) [US/ME/C 1-3]
1800 Hancock Co census ext (NEHGR 105/3-4); Kennebec Co census ext (NEHGR 145/4) [*both* US/NE/PER]

Maryland (MD)
1800 DC census (NGSQ 38/4-39/2) [US/PER]

Massachusetts (MA)
1779 MA census (NGSQ 49/1-3, 50/1,50/4-51/1) [US/PER]
1790 MA census [US/MA/C 1]; Rehoboth census [US/MA/L 43]
1800 Rehoboth census [US/MA/L 43]
1850 Dukes Co census (sailors in ports) (NGSQ 74/4) [US/PER]
1855 MA census ext (twins & oddities) (Nexus 7/2) [US/NE/PER]; MA census ext (Nova Scotians) (NS Gengst 13/3) [CAN/NS/PER]
1860 Chelsea City, Chelsea, N & Winthrop cens [Mf 948]
1865 MA census ext (twins & oddities) (Nexus 7/2) [US/NE/PER]; MA census ext (Nova Scotians) (NS Gengst 13/3) [CAN/NS/PER]
1880 Boston census ext (Newfoundland born) (NL Ancestor 6/4) [CAN/NL/PER]

Michigan (MI)
1762 Detroit: Le Faubourg Ste Rosalie census (Detroit Soc Gencal Res Mag 43/4) [US/MI/PER]
1765 Detroit census (Detroit Soc Gencal Res Mag 43/1) [US/MI/PER]
1787-89 Detroit rets & provisioning lists [CAN/ON/G 8]
1796 Detroit census (NGSQ 69/3) [US/PER]
1810 Detroit dist, MI Terr census (Detroit Soc Gencal Res Mag 32/1) [US/MI/PER]; Michilimackinac, MI Terr census (Detroit Soc Gencal Res Mag 34/3) [US/MI/PER]
1845 Eaton Co census (Detroit Soc Gencal Res Mag 36/1-4) [US/MI/PER]; Oakland Co census [US/MI/C 2]
1860 Raisin census (Detroit Soc Gencal Res Mag 34/1-33/1) [US/MI/PER]
1884 Greenfield census (Detroit Soc Gencal Res Mag 44/2-46/3) [US/MI/PER]
1894 Dickinson Co census (Detroit Soc Gencal Res Mag 42/1-4 & 43/2 incomplete) [US/MI/PER]

Mississippi (MS)
1816 Adams Co census (NGSQ 37/4-38/3); Amite Co, MS Terr census (NGSQ 34/1-2 - *part 1 missing*) [*both* US/PER]
1840-60 MS census exts [US/G 28]
1850 Pontotoc Co census (Dallas Lib Loc Hist & Genlgy Soc 6/2) [US & CAN PER BOX]
1880 Union Co census ext (Dallas Lib Loc Hist & Genlgy Soc 7/4) [US/TX/PER]

Missouri (MO)
1776 St Louis census (St Louis Gencal Q 9/1) [US/MO/PER]
1840-60 MO census exts [US/G 28]
1850 Jackson Co census ext (blacksmiths) (KS City Gengst 32/2) [US/MO/PER]

Nevada (NV)
1870 Gold Hill census ext (English born) [US/NV/C 1]

113

New Hampshire (NH)
1776   NH Association Test [US/NH/C 1]
1790   NH census [US/NH/C 3]
1800   NH census [US/NH/C 2]

New Jersey (NJ)
1800   Cumberland Co census (Gencal Mag NJ 52/3-54/1) [US/NJ/PER]

New York (NY)
1673   Hempstead census [US/NY/G 22]
1689   Ulster Co census [US/NY/G 22]
1698   Newtown census (Am Gengst 24/3) [US/PER]; New Utrecht census (J Long Island Hist 14/1) [US/NY/PER]; Southampton census [US/NY/G 22]
c1698   Southold census [US/NY/G 22]
1702   Orange Co census [US/NY/G 22]
c1703   New York City census [US/NY/G 22]
1706   Staten Is census [US/NY/G 11]
c1708   Staten Is census ext (Am Gengst 36/2) [US/PER]
1714   Dutchess Co census [US/NY/G 22]
1720   Albany City & Co censuses [US/NY/G 22]
1771   Cumberland Co census (Branches & Twigs 8/3) [US & CAN PER BOX]; New Rochelle census (NY Record 107/4) [US/NY/PER]; Newtown census (NY Record 117/1) [US/NY/PER]
1778   Suffolk Co census (NGSQ 63/4) [US/PER or (NY Record 104/4 & 107/2) US/NY/PER]
1790   NY census [US/NY/C 1]; Catharine census [US/NY/L 2]
1800   Amsterdam census (NY Record 50/3) [US/NY Record PER BOX]; Carmel census (NY Record 66/4) [US/NY Record PER BOX]; Catharine census & 1855 [US/NY/L 2]; Charlestown census (NY Record 50/3) [US/NY Record PER BOX]; Florida census (NY Record 50/3) [US/NY Record PER BOX]; Frederick census (NY Record 66/4) [US/NY Record PER BOX]; Mayfield census (NY Record 50/3) [US/NY Record PER BOX]; Minisink census (NY Record 63/1 incomplete) [US/NY Record PER BOX]; Salisbury census (NY Record 50/3) [US/NY Record PER BOX]
1835   Townsendville census (Am Gengst 52/3) [US/PER]
1850   Albany census ext (missing pages) (NY Record 117/3) [US/NY/PER]; Saratoga Co census ext (NGSQ 34/4) [US/PER]
1855   Catharine census [US/NY/L 2]
1860   Gilboa census ext (missing pages) (NY Record 117/2) [US/NY/PER]

North Carolina (NC)
1800-80   NC census exts [US/G 28]
1850   NC census ext (Nova Scotia born) (NS Gengst 2/1) [CAN/NS/PER]; Bladen Co census ext (NGSQ 31/3) [US/PER]; Cumberland Co census Agricultural Schedule (NC Gencal Soc J 14/1 & 3 *incomplete*) [US/NC/PER]

Ohio (OH)
1820   Greene Co census ext (NGSQ 26/4) [US/PER]; Trumbull Co census [US/OH/C 1]
1850   Brown Co census ext (Rota-Gene 14/6) [US/PER]
1863   Belmont Co census ext (blacks) (NGSQ 69/3) [US/PER]
1900   Hamilton Co census ext (Buried Treasures 17/3) [US/FL/PER]

Oklahoma (OK)
1890   OK & Indian Terr census ext (Union veterans & wives) (OK Gencal Soc Bull 4/4-5/2 *incomplete*) [US/OK/PER]

Oregon (OR)
1850 OR Terr census [US Tracts]; Yamhill Co pioneer families (*vols 1-5*) (Forum 14/7-38/4) [US/OR/PER]
1854 Benton Co, OR Terr census (Forum 19/3-6) [US/OR/PER]
1856 Polk Co census [US/OR/C 1]

Pennsylvania (PA)
1790 PA census [US/PA/C 1]; Washington Co census [US/G 145]
1810 Mifflin Township census (Searcher 4/10-12) [US/CA/PER]
1899 Loretto census [US/PA/L 3]

Rhode Island (RI)
1782 RI census (NEHGR 127/1-129/4) [US/NE/PER]
1790 RI census [US/RI/C 1]

South Carolina (SC)
1790 SC census [US/SC/C 1]; Orangeburg census (NGSQ 73/3) [US/PER]
1800-50 SC census exts [US/G 28]

Tennessee (TN)
1830-60 TN census exts [US/G 28]
1850 Franklin Co census ext (Irish railroad builders) (NGSQ 57/1) [US/PER]

Texas (TX)
1826 Austin's Colony census (NGSQ 45/2 & 4) [US/PER]
1829 Tenaha dist census (NGSQ 40/4-41/2) [US/PER]
1834 Nacogdoches census (NGSQ 41/2-3, 42/1-2 & 43/3) [US/PER]
1835 Bevil dist census (NGSQ 42/2-43/1); Sabine dist census (NGSQ 43/3-4 & 44/2-3) [*both* US/PER]
1850 Navarro Co census [US/TX/L 1]
1850-80 TX census exts [US/G 28]
1860 Evergreen census (Stirpes 9/4-10/2) [US/TX/PER]; Navarro Co census [US/TX/L 1]
1870 McCulloch Co census ext (Stirpes 3/3) [US/TX/PER]

Utah (UT)
1851 Davis Co census (UT Gencal & Hist Mag 28/2-29/1); Great Salt Lake Co census (*incomplete*) (UT Gencal & Hist Mag 29/3-4); Iron Co census (UT Gencal & Hist Mag 29/3) [*all* US/UT/PER]

Vermont (VT)
1771 Putney census [US/VT/R 1]; Windham Co cen: see Cumberland Co, New York
1790 VT census [US/VT/C 1]; VT families 1791 (*vol 1*) [US/VT/C 2]
1791 Putney census [US/VT/R 1]
1800 Putney census [US/VT/R 1]
1810 Putney census [US/VT/R 1]; Rutland Co census ext (Am Gengst 45/2) [US/PER]
1820 Putney census [US/VT/R 1]
1830 Putney census [US/VT/R 1]
1840 Putney census [US/VT/R 1]
1850 Chittenden Co census ext (Branches & Twigs 8/3) [US & CAN PER BOX]

Virginia (VA)
1623 VA census [US/MIG 46]
1624 VA census [US/MIG 46]
1779 VA census (NGSQ 46/4) [US/PER]

1782 Surry & Sussex Co censuses [US/VA/L 6]
1810 Giles Co census [US Tracts]
1810-60 VA census exts; WV census ext 1810 [*both* US/G 28]
1820 VA census (*summary*) (Mother Lode 8/2) [US/CA/PER]; Tazewell Co census [US Tracts]
1870 White Creek WV cen: *see Boyd Co, Kentucky*

Washington (WA)
1850 OR Terr census [US Tracts]
1860 Clarke Co census (Seattle Gencal Soc Q Bull 20/4 incomplete) [US/WA/PER]

West Virginia (WV): *see Virginia*

Wisconsin (WI)
1850 St Croix Co census [US Tracts]
1870 Ocunto Co (Pishtiogo tp) Heritage Quest No 68 et.seq. [US/PER]

Wyoming (WY)
1850 OR Terr census [US Tracts]
1860 Fort Laramie census (CO Gengst 30/2-31/2) [US/CO/PER]
1870 Fort Laramie census (CO Gengst 24/1-4) [US/CO/PER]

WEST INDIES (WI)

1520-1797 Cuban cen, padron, etc exts [WI/C 1]
1669 Grenada census (Caribbean Hist & Gencal J 4/2) [WI/PER]
1677-78 Montserrat census (Carib 1) [WI/G 2]; Nevis census (Carib 3) [WI/G 3]
1678 St Kitts census (Carib 2) [WI/G 2]
1679-80 Barbados census [US/MIG 46-47]
1707-08 Nevis & St Kitts cens (Carib 3) [WI/G 3]
1715 Barbados census (J Barbados Museum & Hist Soc 4/2-5/2, 5/4-7/2, 7/4-8/1, 8/3, 9/3) [WI/PER]
1716 Anguilla census (Carib 3) [WI/G 3]
1729 Montserrat census (Carib 4) [WI/G 4]
1857 Cuba: Guantanamo padron (Caribbean Hist & Gencal J 4/2) [WI/PER]

APPENDIX - GENERAL REFERENCE BOOKS AND FINDING AIDS

1. ENGLAND and WALES
1851 census index survey for England, Wales and Channel Islands - C. McLee (1992) [MLC]
Beginning Genealogy, Part 3: English and Welsh census returns 1841-1891 - Arthur Dark (1997) [TB/FH]
The census and how to use it - J. Borham (1992) [MLC]
Census 1841 reference book: HO 107/1-1465 class lists [England, Wales, Channel Islands and Isle of Man] [MLC]
Census 1851 reference book: HO 107/1466-2531 class lists [England, Wales, Isle of Man, Jersey and Guernsey [MLC]
Census 1861 reference book: RG 9/1-4543 class lists [England, Wales, Channel Islands, Isle of Man, and British ships in home ports [MLC]
Census 1891 reference book: RG 12/1-4708 class lists [England, Wales, Channel Islands, Isle of Man [MLC]
Census returns 1841-1881 in microform: A directory of local holdings in Great Britain; Channel Islands; Isle of Man - Elizabeth Hampson and Jeremy Gibson (1994) [Quick Reference Shelves - Gibson Guides binder]
Censuses and census taking 1801-1901 - E. Higgs (1996) [Audio cassette rack]
A clearer sense of the census. The Victorian census and historical research: Public Record Office Handbooks no. 28 - E. Higgs (1996) [TB/RG]
English Census Street Indexes - LONDON (Descent 16/2) [AUA/PER]
Genealogy in Early British Censuses - C. Chapman in Anglo Celtic Annals. Proceedings of the BIFHSGO Conference (1997) [CAN/ON/PER]
Guide to census reports: Great Britain 1801-1966 [TB/RG]
Index to census registration districts (including the 1891 lists) - M E Bryant Rosier (1992) [Apply to staff shelf 8]
Instructions for the 1881 census of England, Wales, Channel Islands and Isle of Man - Genealogical Society of Utah (1992) [Lower Library]
An introduction to ... Census Returns of England and Wales - S. Lumas (1992) [TB/RG]
Local census listings 1522-1930: Holdings in the British Isles - J S W Gibson and M Medlycott (1992) [Quick reference shelves - Gibson Guides binder]
Local communities in the Victorian census enumerator's books - eds D. Mills and K. Schürer
Making sense of the census. The manuscript returns for England and Wales, 1801-1901. Public Record Office handbooks no. 23 - E. Higgs (1989) [TB/RG]
Making use of the census: Public Record Office readers' guide no. 1 - S. Lumas (1997) [TB/RG and SP/PER]
Marriage census and other indexes for family historians - Elizabeth Hampson and J S W Gibson (1996) [Quick reference shelves - Gibson Guides binder]
Place name index to the 1891 census vols 1-11 - M E MacSorley (1997) [TB/RG]
Pre 1841 census and population listings in the British Isles - C. Chapman (1994) [TB/RG]
The use of census enumeration districts in the study of Irish immigrants in the St. Martin's district of Liverpool in the mid-19th century - L. Letford [Audio cassette rack]

2. IRELAND
Census of Ireland 1851 - General Alphabetical Index to the Townlands and Towns of Ireland [TB Quick Ref]
Census of Ireland 1871 - Alphabetical Index to the Townlands and Towns of Ireland [IR/C 1]
1766 Religious Census of Ireland [IR/G 182]
Ireland Old Age Pension Claims - An introduction to the Claims & Guide to the Name Index [Apply to Staff (Shelf 9)]

3. SCOTLAND
An act for taking the census of England 6th August, 1860, Scotland 10th August, 1870 to provide the early notification of

117

Births (28th August 1907) to extend the Notification of Births Act 1907 [MLC]
Census returns & old parochial registers on microfilm. A directory of public library holdings in the West of Scotland [MLC shelf 9]
Census records for Scottish families at home & abroad [SC/C 6]
Scottish census indexes covering 1841-71 civil censuses [Apply to Staff Shelf 9]
West of Scotland Census returns & OPRs [Apply to Staff Shelf 9]

4. OVERSEAS
a. CANADA
Catalogue of Census Returns on Microfilm 1666-1891 (Public Archives of Canada) [CAN/C 1]
Pre-1851 Census Records of Ontario (Gencal J 13/2) [US/UT/PER]

b. DENMARK
Danish Census Records (Heritage Quest 19) [US/PER]

c. UNITED STATES OF AMERICA - FEDERAL
Availability of Federal Population Census Schedules in the States (NGSQ 50/1-2 & 51/1) [US/PER]
Availability of Name Indexes to Federal Population Census Schedules 1790-1890 (NGSQ 51/3) [US/PER]
City, County, Town and Township Index to the 1850 Federal Census Schedules (Gale Genealogy & Local History Series vol 6) [US/C 3]
Encyclopedia of Local History and Genealogy ser 1 vol 2; Census Encyclopedia [US/C 6]
Federal Population Censuses, 1790-1890; a catalogue of microfilm copies of the schedules [US/C 2]
The "Forgotten" Census of 1880: Defective, Dependent and Delinquent Classes (NGSQ 80/1) [US/PER]
Map Guide to the Federal Censuses 1790-1920 [US/C 5]
US Census Key 1850, 1860, 1870 [US/C 1]
US Census Oddities with emphasis on defunct counties (Gencal J 11/2) [US/PER]
US Research Outlines: see Federal & State entries under 'Census' [US/G 121]

d. UNITED STATES OF AMERICA - STATES
New York State and Federal Census Records (Heritage Quest 9) [US/PER]
State Census Records [US/C 4]
The State Censuses of NY 1825-75 (Gencal J 14/4) [US/PER]
Using State Census Records (Copper State Bull 24/4) [US/AZ/PER]